TO SNUFFY
(the first Helmsdale dominie)

TO HAMISH
(his son)

and to their descendants.

DUNROBIN CASTLE from a painting by Daniell, c 1820

ACKNOWLEDGMENTS

This book is the result of a suggestion by my wife, Betty, that I use the records of the late James Campbell, sometime dominie at Helmsdale, to tell others how he had seen life there in the late 19th, and early 20th centuries. This has only been accomplished with her continuing support, and with the help given by very many people, none more so than Miss A. S. Cowper, Edinburgh who has been unstinting in her assistance in so many ways.

Many others have also given very, very. willingly of their assistance. These include the Countess of Sutherland and Lord Strathnaver; from Helmsdale and district, Mr A I Blance, Mrs M Dudgeon, Mrs E O Fraser, Mr Gordon Gordon, Miss B M Innes, Mr J Jappy, Mr A Jappy, Mr D McAngus, Miss M MacGregor, Mr G MacKenzie, Mrs M MacKenzie, Sir Anthony Nutting (Bt.), Auchentoul Estate; Mrs Margaret Polson, Mr J Sutherland, Mr & Mrs J. Sutherland, Mr Francis Traill, Sir Michael Wigan (Bt.), Borrobol Estate: from Brora Mr J MacLennan, and from Littleferry, Mr J G Henderson.

From further afield, help has come from Professor R J Adam, St Andrews; Mr Jens Bagh, Calgary; Mr Geoffrey Baggott, London; Dr Malcolm Bangor-Jones, Dundee; Mrs Catherine Burns, Inverness; Mrs Linda Bankier, Berwick on Tweed Borough Council; Professor Barrow, Edinburgh; Mr & Mrs J Corkill, Largs; Dr James Coull, University of Dundee; Allan M Carswell, Scottish United Services Museum; Miss Liza Farrelly, Wick Archivist; Mrs O M Geddes, National Library of Scotland; Ms Morna Gerrard and Miss A. Lindsay, SRO.; Miss Christine Lodge, Inverness Archivist's Dept; Mr Kevin McLaren, RCAHMS, Edinburgh; Ms Seonaid MacDonald, Bank of Scotland Archivist; Mr Peter Milne, Map Room, Scottish National Library; Dr J A Morrison, Aberdeen; Mr R Pedersen, Inverness; Ms Helen Redmond-Cooper, Bank of Scotland Archivist; Mr Ian Simpson, Aberdeen; Mr Robert Steward, Inverness Archivist; and Miss Diana Wright, Berwick-on-Tweed Borough Council.

Nor can I praise too highly the co-operation I have had from the staff of the Largs Branch of the North Ayrshire Authority, who have succeeded in obtaining for me all the reference works I sought.

DUKES, EARLS, and COUNTESSES OF SUTHERLAND

Succesion
Date
c.1211 Freskin The Fleming;
      Followed by William son of Freskin;
      and Hugh son of William;
1235 William son of Hugh, First Earl of Sutherland;
1248 William, Second Earl of Sutherland;
c.1306 William, Third Earl of Sutherland;
c.1330 Kenneth, Fourth Earl of Sutherland;
1333 William, Fifth Earl of Sutherland;
1389 Robert, Sixth Earl of Sutherland, Dunrobin Castle
      mentioned for first time;
c.1427 John, Seventh Earl of Sutherland;
c.1455 John, Eighth Earl of Sutherland; (Mentally ill)
1494 John, Ninth Earl of Sutherland; (Mentally ill)
1514 Elizabeth, Countess of Sutherland;
1537 John, Tenth Earl of Sutherland; (Poisoned at Helmsdale.)
1567 Alexander, Eleventh Earl of Sutherland;
1594 John, Twelfth Earl of Sutherland;
1615 John, Thirteenth Earl of Sutherland;
1679 George, Fourteenth Earl of Sutherland;
1703 John, Fifteenth Earl of Sutherland;
1734 William, Sixteenth Earl of Sutherland;
1750 William, Seventeenth Earl of Sutherland;
1766 Elizabeth, Countess of Sutherland from age of 1 year;
1833 George, First Duke of Sutherland.
1833 George, Second Duke and Eighteenth Earl of Sutherland;
1861 George, Third Duke and Nineteenth Earl of Sutherland.
1892 Cromartie, Fourth Duke and Twentieth Earl of Sutherland;
1913 George, Fifth Duke of Sutherland and Twenty First Earl of
      Sutherland;
1963 John, Sixth Duke of Sutherland;
1963 Elizabeth, Twenty Fourth Countess of Sutherland.

Note:-The Dukedom and Earldom were held by same person until the death
of 5th Duke and 22nd Earl without issue. Then, as the Earldom could pass
by female line, and the Dukedom could not, the two titles separated.

CONTENTS

PREFACE

Someone has said that the history we forget we are condemned to repeat. A work such as Duncan Campbell's 'Some Helmsdale Memories' fixes the subject of the east coast Sutherland village of Helmsdale in time, and provides a proper base for those whose footsteps must follow. Simply, it is essential for Highland people to know more than how this famous little village arose —from the Sutherland Clearances — but also how it developed; and it is enriching for anyone else interested in Scottish affairs.

Helmsdale is a place with a larger significance than its present population would suggest. Not only did it become around the turn of the century one of the Scottish herring fishery's major ports, but it has always been a place, both on the land side and the seaward one, despite its northerly latitude, rich in natural resources. The author's figures illustrate this. His mid nineteenth century tables of exports from Helmsdale show often prodigious quantities of barley, wool, salmon, and barrelled herrings going south and across the sea to the east, and later on large quantities of lobsters, crabs and assorted fish. There is no figure, in the nature of things, for what the Kildonan Gold Rush, a century ago, yielded up in total. It is a teasing speculation. But clearly God smiled on this faraway place and provided a gold resource too.

Today sheepmeat, beef, timber and venison will have replaced some of the earlier commodities, whilst the village has gained a reputation for cultural enthusiasm, with its brilliantly imaginative Timespan Heritage Centre (a concept which quickly became a trend-setter) and its prestigious Highland Games, now attracting big crowds and some of the more buoyant names in athletic competition.

Duncan Campbell's scrupulously accurate, carefully detailed, and whimsically told account puts flesh on the bones of many a fading name, often using humorous anecdote. Some details, such as fishermen carrying a sharp knife with which to slice off their seaboots if they fell in, whilst other more realistically-minded colleagues deliberately never learned to swim to save themselves a futile struggle against the cruel elements, bring to life times past and the toughness needed for ordinary survival. Perhaps above all in this respect, in depicting the harsh actualities of existence only a short time ago, his book deserves to be read and its historical lessons noted.

Though a small place Helmsdale lays fair claim to being unlike anywhere else. No 'Helmie' would care to be mistaken for a denizen of Caithness, nor yet of the rival town Brora. On the westward side there is no village until the western seaboard, a fact which has maybe contributed to Helmsdale's development of notable character. This sense of community is strong (those who make their way in the wider world have a tendency faithfully to return and lend a helping hand) and Duncan Campbell, with his powerful local connections as the grandson of the dominie mentioned in the text, is the correct person to present this commendable record.

Michael Wigan

Borrobol,
Kinbrace,
Sutherland.

I INTRODUCTION

In the early 19th century many noble households squandered large inheritances. For example Lord Reay, Caithness lost his whole estate overnight at the gambling tables in London. In the case of the Sutherlands, however, a large proportion of their wealth was used to benefit their estates and, in so doing, the lot of the local inhabitants. This latter aspect involved not only improving communications, but also, in the longer term, living conditions.

In Sutherlandshire the work done resulted in communication improvements which upgraded the road system out of all recognition, and also brought the railway to the area. The latter scheme both improved future trading prospects, and relieved the hardships of 1870.

Other measures introduced to benefit the local inhabitants included work at Brora to improve the coal mine, starting an engineering workshop there, as well as carpet factories at Embo, Lybster and Helmsdale. Loans were made to fishermen to purchase new boats, and large sums were laid out on planned villages at Helmsdale and at Brora.

Finance for all this work was only available because, in 1803, the Marquess of Stafford, husband of Elizabeth, Countess of Sutherland, later to be made 1st Duke of Sutherland for political services, inherited a very large annual income from his uncle, the Duke of Bridgewater. This was in the form of canal profits. The Marquess decided to use a large part of this legacy to upgrade his wife's Sutherland estate whilst at the same time seeking to improve the estate's profitability. This he wanted to do by converting to sheep farms the large tracts of the land then occupied by many small tenants mostly involved in cattle rearing. Just how necessary it was to improve the road system will be appreciated when it is realised that up to that time there was only one bridge in the whole estate of 1,250 square miles. This was at Brora and was used to convey coal from the mine to the harbour. There were no roads at all capable of handling wheeled traffic.

He seems to have been very badly advised about the conversion of the land to the raising of sheep and also about the men to carry it into operation. This involved the large scale eviction of tenants which, in many cases, was carried out in an outrageous and inhuman fashion, especially during the period 1810 - 1825. This resulted in hundreds of local Sutherland people emigrating to Canada and New Zealand. Those remaining, with great

11

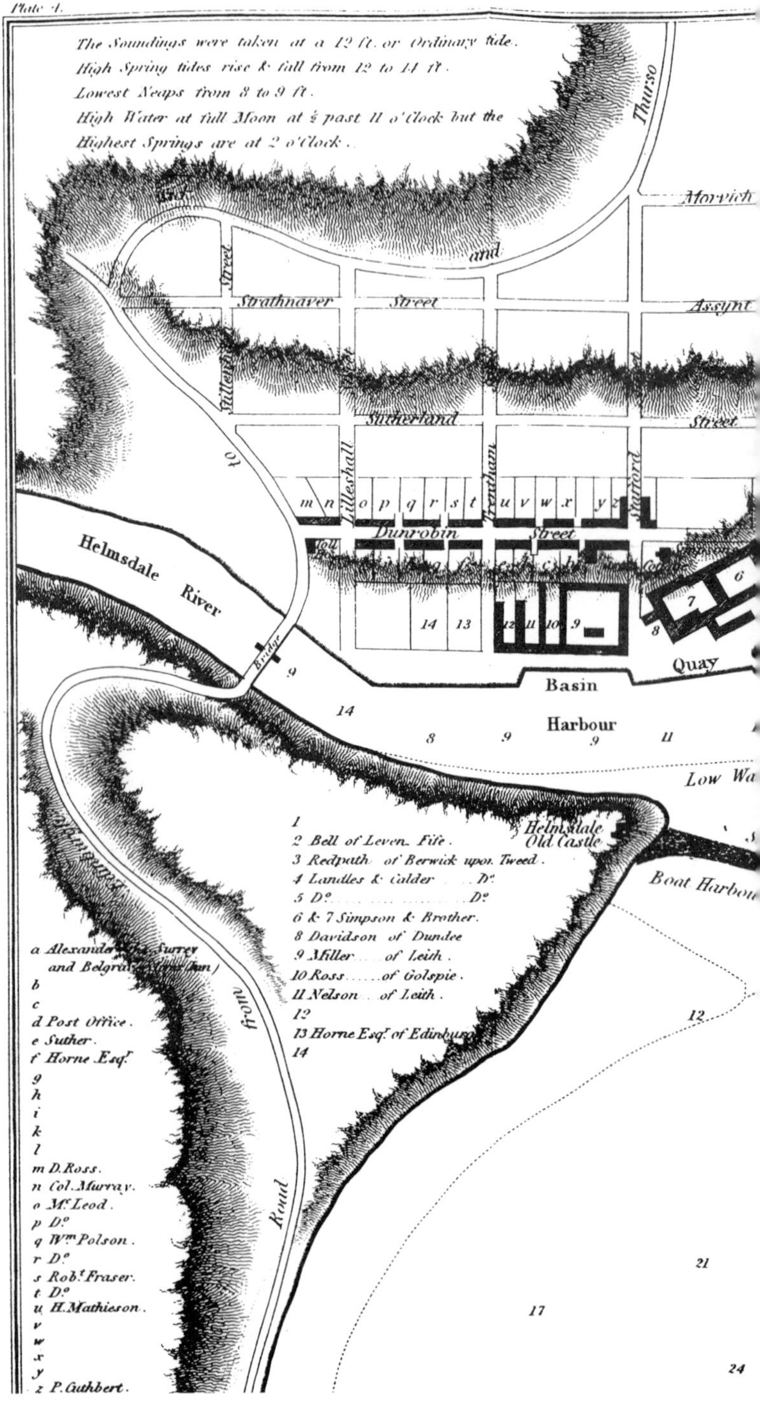

Plate 4.

The Soundings were taken at a 12 ft. or Ordinary tide.
High Spring tides rise & fall from 12 to 14 ft.
Lowest Neaps from 8 to 9 ft.
High Water at full Moon at ½ past 11 o'Clock but the
Highest Springs are at 2 o'Clock.

Thurso

Morvich

Street

and

Strathnaver   Street   Assynt

Sutherland   Street

m n o p q r s t u v w x y z

Dunrobin   Street

Helmsdale   River

14 13   12 11 10 9

Bridge
9

14   Quay

Basin

8   9   Harbour
                        9   11

Low Wa

1
2 Bell of Leven. Fife.
3 Redpath of Berwick upon Tweed.   Helmsdale
4 Landles & Calder .... Dº.   Old Castle
5 Dº. .... Dº.
6 & 7 Simpson & Brother.
8 Davidson of Dundee.   Boat Harbour
a Alexander   Surrey   9 Miller of Leith.
   and Belgrave   (   )   10 Ross ...... of Golspie.
b   11 Nelson .... of Leith.
c   12
d Post Office.   13 Horne Esqʳ of Edinburgh   12
e Suther.   14
f Horne Esqʳ
g
h
i
k
l
m D. Ross.
n Col. Murray.
o McLeod.
p Dº.
q Wm Polson.
r Dº.   21
s Robt Fraser.
t Dº.
u H. Mathieson.   17
v
w
x
y   24
z P. Cuthbert.

12

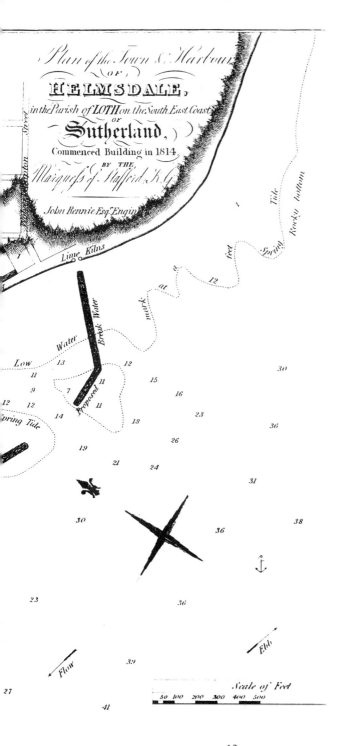

Fig. No. 1.

First proposal for layout of Helmsdale Streets and harbour and put into operation in 1814. By Courtesy of Sutherland Estates.

13

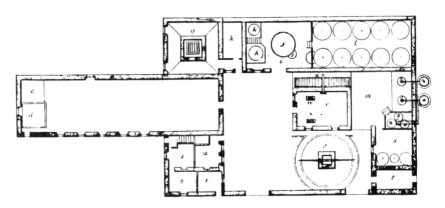
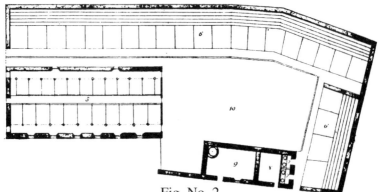

a Workmens Barracks, d? above
b Couch, Cistern above
c Malt house, Barley loft above
d Cistern
e Couch
f Malt house, Barley loft above
g Kiln
h Spirit cellar, Malt store above
i Mash house, Wort Receiver d?
j Mash Tun and under back
k Coppers
l Tun Room with 10 Fermenting Tuns Coolers above
m Still house
n Wash Still and Condenser
o Lowine Still and condenser
p Lowine Receiver
q Spirit Receiver
r Wort Receiver

s Spirit cellar with 3 spirit Vats
t Draff house
u Water Wheel
v Malt Mill, Malt deposit above
w Machinery driven by water wheel
x d? d? by horse wheel
y Horse wheel
z Excise Office
1 Counting Room
2 Managers Bedroom
3 d? Kitchen with 2 apartments above
4 Garden
5 Feeding Byre
6 Piggery
7 Privy
8 Hen house
9 Workshop with boiler
10 Dung Pit

Fig. No. 2.

Plans of Helmsdale Distillery.
By Courtesy of Sutherland Estates.

14

fortitude, created new livelihoods in coastal areas such as Helmsdale, but endured initially the most abject poverty and deprivation.

Obviously the expenditure involved was massive, and whilst an Exchequer contribution of 50% of approved outlays was available this only applied to the main roads, or in the Sutherland case about 90 miles out of the overall total of 500 miles.

Besides the road works there were constructed the Telford Bridge at Helmsdale, (costing £2,200), one hundred and thirty four other bridges, and two chain ferries for river crossings considered too long to bridge.

When allied to the complementary schemes for inns and stabling at Clashmore, Golspie and Portgower, and a post office at Dornoch, these improvements enabled the Estate to persuade the Post Office to extend the Royal Mail northward from Inverness. Consequently, although it was to be a further ten years before all the bridges were in place, by 1819 stage coaches were travelling through Helmsdale up to Wick and other north coast towns, and so Helmsdale became a convenient resting place for horses and travellers either about to tackle the stresses of the Ord with its exposed roads and steep inclines, or to rest from their after effects.

Before the new roadworks began, there were only a small inn and a few cottages round the mouth of the Helmsdale river for those who were working on the nearby salmon boiling and pickling plant. In 1762 the inn was described by the Right Reverend Robert Forbes as having "a little snug garden made out of the Greatest Wild with his own hand; in which we saw Gooseberries, Apples, the hundred-leaf'd Rose, White Lillies,...Firs, Ash, Beech, Oak...and Cauliflowers" He also mentions that "the sea flows up at Tides" almost to the inn door and that "At the mouth of the water of the Helmsdale there is good Salmon-Fishing, plenty of trout, and a Safe Inlet for Fishing". On another journey he mentions that he "dined at Helmsdale on Mutton-Collaps, and new baked Salmon".

To cope with the additional work the Sutherland Estates required additional staff in the factor's office. Amongst those engaged was an 18th century "whiz kid", William Young, who had made a success of a similar situation on his own smaller estate near Elgin.

During an inspection of the construction work on the bridge, William Young focused on the possibilities of developing the surrounding area commercially, and reported to the then Marquess in 1810 that "Helmsdale seems well adapted for a Fishing Station both from its local situation, and,

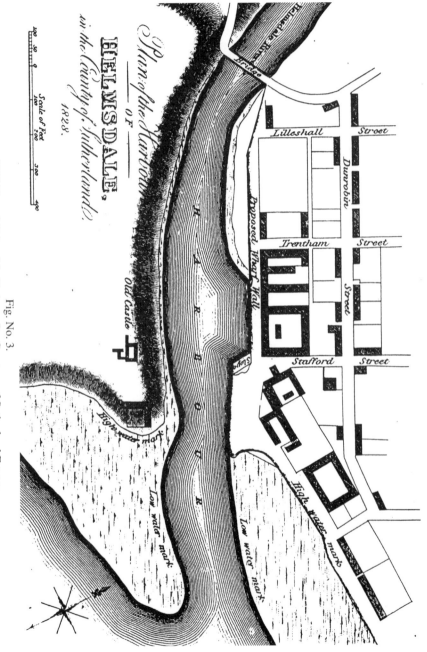

Fig. No. 3.
1828 Plan of Helmsdale Harbour. By Courtesy of Sutherland Estates.

16

as the adjoining sea is known to contain Cod, Ling, Haddocks, and other white fish, here the Moray Firth Fishermen frequently come to set their lines. Immediate steps should be taken to get possession of some ground suitable for a Village and to induce Fishermen from the south side to settle at this place".

At the time of Mr Young's report, the major part of the land there was held by Lord Hermand in wadset (a type of loan/lease arrangement) so, whilst it was 1816 before full legal access could be gained to the major part of the targeted area, construction of this new planned village had commenced in 1814 and it was not long before expenditure of around £20 million in 1990 terms had provided the start of the neat streets of houses we see today, as well as a fish curing shed, and then, later, a distillery and a carpet factory.

A plan of how it was intended the village would be laid out is contained in Fig. 1. From this it will be seen that the area round the harbour was built, but not all of the projected streets. As well as developments on land the number of fishing boats based at Helmsdale had risen from 20 in 1814, to 204 in 1819.

Before the bridge was built, the river was crossed at a ford. Near this, in the west part of what is now the cemetery, had stood in early times a chapel and hospice dedicated to St John the Baptist - on the north side of the river there still stands St John's Well. This chapel was known locally as the Church of Kiliain.

Just below this point is the "Coach Pool", traditionally so called because a coach allegedly was swept into it off the ford and all the passengers drowned. It is probably also the "St John's Puile" of 1558.

The 3rd Duke had a passionate interest in railways, but the operating companies were very slow in pushing the track northwards from Inverness. Perhaps this is not altogether surprising considering both the civil engineering problems involved, and the lack (at that time) of obvious traffic for the line, but, through his efforts and influence, the track reached Helmsdale by 1870, bringing with it many benefits to the locality.

The fishing industry became the mainstay of what was at times a very prosperous 19th century village community. This is confirmed from Tables F and J, which show that in the "peak" years 38037 barrels of herring and 1005 boxes of salmon were exported.

There was also revenue from crofting activities, from sporting tenants,

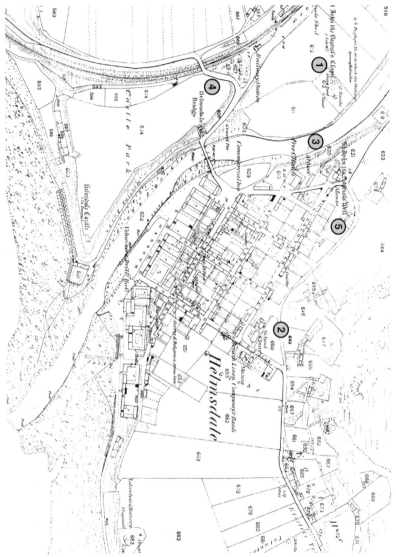

Fig. No. 4.
Map Showing Helmsdale Inner Harbour, Jetty, and Location of Churches. Point No. 1 Site of former Church of Kiliain; Point No. 2 Former Parish Church of St John; Point No. 3 Free Church of Scotland; Point No. 4 Former Free Presbyterian Church; Point No. 5 Former United Free Church of Scotland, now Bunillidh Church of Scotland.

18

Fig. No. 5.

Photograph showing harbour groynes (Point 1), as well as original Free Church and school (Point 2).
Reproduced with permission from the George Washington Wilson Collection, Aberdeen University Library

and, on a short-term basis, from the discovery of gold in the nearby hills. Neither the distillery nor the carpet factory was so successful. The distillery opened its doors in 1825, and changed hands twice before going bankrupt in 1840. Perhaps this is not altogether surprising as a 40 gallon still was discovered in Strathcarron in 1905, and there is evidence of illegal distilling taking place not too far from the village as late as 1910! Incidentally the last surviving portion of spirit produced at the distillery can be seen in Timespan Heritage Centre.

After it closed, the plant was stripped out, and the buildings shown in the 1831 plan (in Fig. 2) became first an isolation hospital, then fishermen's cottages and latterly stores for herring barrels. The carpet factory which opened in 1905, and of which more details are given in Chapter V, closed about four years later.

The format of the harbour was altered from time to time to accommodate the increase in the number of boats. Though breastwork was done in 1818, the stages of visible evidence are first the wharf wall of 1828 (see Fig.3), then the inner harbour (shown in Fig. 4), and finally the outer harbour, the foundation stone of which was laid in 1892 by the "Harbour Trust". Between the two latter stages a number of groynes were erected as shown in Fig. 5, whilst a movable boom to protect the inner harbour had been added in 1909.

Basically life in Helmsdale in the nineteenth century was controlled by the dictates of Sutherland Estates, with a combination of the local minister, schoolmaster and doctor providing the main leadership within the growing community. Unfortunately, the timings of the various schisms in the Church caused such deep divides that ministers and members of the different denominations were often quite unable to work together. The gap this created was filled by the very shrewd and public-spirited Couper family, helped by the slightly authoritarian behaviour of the local police force in their administration of justice. Sometimes this was administered in the spirit of the legislation in preference to the letter of it!

Local government came in the nineteenth century with the Parochial Boards (1845) and the County Councils (1890) when the first meeting of Sutherland County Council was held in the drill hall, Bonar Bridge after a provisional meeting had been held in the Sheriff Court Room, Dornoch. In the twentieth century came Regionalisation (1975) and finally Unitary Authorities.

The 1914-18 war changed life in many respects. The influence of the Estate and the Church decreased and democratic attitudes developed.

II. ANTIQUITIES

The name Helmsdale is thought to have its origins in the ninth century when the area was overrun by Norse invaders, in whose sagas occurs the name "Hailmisdaill" or "Hjalmunsdal" (the dale of the tiller).

The area round Helmsdale has been inhabited by man for a very, very long time. If any proof of this is needed, it can be found in the listings by the Royal Commission of Ancient and Historical Monuments of over a hundred sites of possible archaeological interest which lie in the area broadly bounded by Berridale, Braemore, Altanduin and Brora. Most of these are still unrecorded in detail, but one that is reasonably accessible is a broch near Caen, where at least three underground chambers can be traced.

The Romans also seem to have known the river as can be deduced both from the artefacts they left behind as noted below, and also from the appearance of the river as "Ila fluvius" in the 2nd century maps by the Greek cartographer Ptolemy which were based on Roman Navy surveys.

In the area which is now covered by the village, several very old graves containing skeletons enclosed within flat stones were found during building operations. Three of them were found when a start was made to levelling the ground in front of Bunillidh Cottage in old Caithness Road. Another was found on the level ground above the cottage to the north of it, and yet another when the foundations of the school gymnasium were excavated.

Naturally when the major engineering works were being undertaken in connection with the railway, other items came to light. These (and others) may be briefly listed as follows:-

1. On Ben Griam, about 2 miles along the road from Kinbrace, two stones were discovered with some sculpting on them. These are thought to have gone to the museum at Dunrobin Castle.

2. When the foundation was being excavated for the addition to the original room at Helmsdale School, Roman coins were discovered. Some other Roman coins and five bronze bowls, (one in the unique form of a strainer) probably of Roman origin were also found at the approach to Helmsdale station.

3. Where the doctor's house now stands at the junction with the Strath road, was the "Heather Inn". When this was being demolished, the workmen came across an ornate fireplace, the discovery of which was immediately reported to Dr Joass - a keen antiquarian who was a minister in

Golspie.Early the next morning, Dr Joass drove up from Golspie (overlooking the fact it was Sunday and he should have been taking a service) and decided it must have come from Helmsdale Castle. It was first taken to Dunrobin Castle, but has now been incorporated in the "Timespan" building.

4. In 1872 a stone of some interest was discovered on Ben Griam. "Robert Ormiston who with David McKay were the only parties who saw it...[and described it as being]....about 2ft long and 18 inches broad and 3 or 4 inches thick...all covered with an inscription of which they could make nothing."

5. Sent to Dr Joass were "three coins found at Cadhain in one of the cairns immediately north of the sheepfold." They had been discovered by some boys out rabbit hunting.

6. In the autumn of 1871 it was reported to Dr Joass that George Sutherland, Marrel, a navvy on the railway, had found a stone bowl of fine workmanship, nine and a quarter inches in circumference round the rim with no markings outside or inside, except two lines partly defaced about the rim. "It is of the blue stone to which you referred."

7. Of comparatively recent discovery is a stone noticed by Dr Scott lying in the garage at the Post Office. This he had thought was Pictish. Sometime later it was taken to the cemetery at Navidale by Mr James Ross of Burnside where it was noticed by an inspector of the Ministry of Building and Works who assumed it had always been there, and arranged it be placed in the museum at Dunrobin Castle, where it still lies. Expert opinion has dated it to about 7th or 8th century A.D. Mr Ross was very interested in the preservation of antiquities and was a close friend of Rev Dr Scott.

The old castle whose ruins were removed in 1972 to allow the building of the new road bridge, seems to have been constructed about 1460 and enlarged about 1600 by Sir Alexander Gordon of Navidale, whose two sons were born there in 1614 and 1616. In 1621, however, because of the clan troubles, Sir Alexander decided to move to Torrish, where he built another castle. Thereafter he abandoned Helmsdale Castle, which gradually became a complete ruin. All that now remains of this once imposing building is a lintel from one of the fireplaces which is built into the structure of "Timespan" referred to above.

Its principal claim to fame lies in the fact that in 1567 it was the site of an attempt by Lady Isobel Sinclair, wife of Gilbert Gordon of Garty, to kill not only his nephew, the Earl of Sutherland and his wife the Countess, but also their 15-year-old, son and heir. Her object was to ensure her son, next in line of succession, would take over the estates. Unfortunately, whilst she succeeded in killing the Earl and Countess, their son escaped, but her own son died by accidentally drinking the same poisoned wine as that already consumed by the Earl and the Countess. Shortly afterwards she died by her own hand, whilst in prison in Edinburgh.   As will be seen from the opening list of the holders of the Earldom/Dukedom of Sutherland, the title is a very old one, dating back to about 1211 when it was conferred on Freskin, of Flemish origin, by William the Lion. For the next four to five hundred years clan wars and skirmishes were waged frequently with the neighbouring territories of the Clans Mackay, Gunn and Sinclair. In addition able-bodied clansmen (the Sutherlands could usually raise up to about 2,000 men) were required to support distant campaigns.

Under the entail of 1705 the title devolved on Elizabeth, the nineteenth in succession, in 1766. She was then an orphan of about two years old, but it was only after legal enquiries that her right to the title was confirmed by a House of Lords' decision in 1771. She married George Granville Leveson-Gower, the Viscount Trentham, who was later to become the wealthy Marquess of Stafford. Later still, as a reward for political services, he became the 1st Duke of Sutherland, but Elizabeth chose to be distinguished as Duchess-Countess of Sutherland. She died in 1838, but, being female, was never "Chief of the Clan", and so not entitled to sport the eagle's feathers.

In a period of twelve days in 1779, a fencible force of 1000 men was raised in her name, and in 1793 another body of "Fencible" clansmen was raised to help with the war against France, but an attempt in 1854 to raise a battalion for the war with Russia, produced not a single enlistment. These fencibles were to become the Sutherland Highlanders, or 93rd Regiment of the line.

The first mention of Dunrobin Castle as the seat of the Sutherland family occurs in 1389, but probably came into existence a few years earlier.

What we see today is a building which was substantially reconstructed between 1844 and 1848 at a cost of about £60,000 (say £25 million in 1990s terms). As such it reflects the elaborate style of landlords of the period, and is open to the public at most times throughout the year.

"Modernised" on several occasions since, it houses a stunning collection of 19th century furniture, family portraits and silverware which reflect the life-style of the family in the 19th century when it was at the height of its power and influence.

The museum which overlooks the lovely gardens presently being redeveloped within the original 1850 design, began life as "Earl William's Summer House", and contains not only family artefacts, but also many items relating to the County of Sutherland.

III THE CHURCH PRIOR TO 1843

Christianity came to the area surrounding the mouth of the Helmsdale river in four different stages. First with the Celtic teachings brought by a Ninianic mission about 390 A.D. which rested at what we now know as Navidale. The very name itself comes from one or two Gaelic sources connected with this event.

One argument is that the Norse "dale" is the suffix to "neamh" which translates as "heaven", the other is that it comes from "nemed" which translates as "sanctuary". On balance the latter is preferred, as in his 17th century Genealogical History of the Earldom of Sutherland, Sir Robert Gordon speaks of Navidale being known as a "sanctuarie". In this connection Ninian's followers liked isolated, high rock positions, or promontories bounded by the sea. The former burial ground includes St Ninian's well and St Ninian's field. The chapel which "was sometime a place of refuge or sancturie" was "demolished and burnt" around 1556 by the Clan Mackay.

St Donan visited the church at Navidale in 580 A.D., before going on to found his own cell at Kildonan - a cell later replaced by rough stone church about 1069, which, with various alterations, lasted until about 1788.

After the Synod of Whitby, the rule of the Celtic Church in Scotland was replaced by the power of Rome with its tendency to operate through religious houses such as monasteries. These also had small outreach chapels and in 1362 we find an entry in the records of the monastery at Kinloss, recording the gift to the monastery of a chapel and a hospice at the mouth of the river Helmsdale by the Earl of Sutherland. This would be to assist travellers, and possibly people on pilgrimages. The chapel was dedicated to St John the Baptist, but was still referred to by its Gaelic name of Kiliain (the cell of Iain) in the 19th century: it lay in the western portion of what is now the graveyard, and is point 1 on the map in Fig. No. 4.

Still in use after the Reformation for Presbyterian worship, and, latterly, with its manse probably in Dunrobin Street on the site of what is now the Community Centre, the Church continued to serve the spiritual needs of the community until 1841. It was too small for the developing community by 1826 when a petition was sent from the Presbytery of Dornoch to the Duchess of Sutherland, asking for the provision of a new building. One of the arguments advanced was that if such was not available some may elect to follow a "dissenting minister".

The argument was accepted, and as a short term measure the Duchess gave the use of a store on the opposite side of the river for use both as a "Chapel of Ease" and as a school. Building operations started in 1835 just two years after her husband had died and of course his inherited legacy income had stopped. These were suspended by the Duchess not long afterwards, allegedly because of "extraordinary interference by Mr Andrew MacKay and some others", but maybe the pause was dictated by the economy drives instituted at that time by James Loch, the estate factor, especially as at that time she was also engaged in the restoration of Dornoch Cathedral. However, a further petition, signed by 128 residents, resulted in the Duchess allowing work to continue. The new Parish Church to replace Kiliain, was dedicated to St John in 1841. Many local residents had raised about £300 (probably about £120,000 in 1990s terms) towards the construction of the new church - much of it in donations of about 2/6d, and even some from registered paupers.

A public outcry had followed the thoughtlessness of the Duchess during the restoration of the cathedral at Dornoch, when she caused about fifty partially decomposed bodies to be dug up, and then taken in a cart to be re-interred without ceremony or respect in a trench dug for the purpose. This act created disillusionment and disgust with Helmsdale church members and elsewhere throughout the county, and probably was an additional factor which influenced the swing to the Free Church in 1843 as a positive protest against the Establishment.

Two pre-Reformation factors left their mark on the parish of Kildonan. One is in the form of place names and the other is in fishing rights. The place names refer to a house and a loch, and both are of the same origin. The house is "Taigh an Abb", and the loch is "Loch an Abb" or Abbot's House and Abbot's Loch respectively. These are linked to the Abbot of Scone having been one of Bishop Murray's Canons for the Bishopric of Caithness c.1222 or c.1225, with charge of Kildonan until the Reformation put an end to medieval church rule.

In the case of the fishing rights, Master Thomas Brodie or Brady, prebendary of Helmsdale, granted to Alexander, Master of Sutherland, lands and crofts of Marrel and salmon fishing of "St John Puile" with cruives, to bear rental of £20 p.a. & 6/8d augmentation in 1558, rights which at a later date the Sutherland Estates had to buy back from the Church.

The basis of the Church established after the Reformation, with the teachings of John Knox, remained reasonably acceptable until 1843.

As communications were so difficult in the late 18th and early 19th centuries, a large part of the keeping of law and order devolved on the local Kirk Session and the minister. We are fortunate that Donald Sage, son of the Rev Alexander Sage, minister of Kildonan from 1787 to 1824, wrote his "Memorabilia" of life in his times in Kildonan and Sutherland. Donald's son published his father's recollections in 1889, and whilst some of his recollections have recently been challenged as a result of impartial historic research, the broad picture he paints of this time is absolutely fascinating.

When the Rev Alexander Sage was appointed on an annual stipend of £70, the church was described as "a small Popish building thatched with heather". In the following year a new church was erected, to a plan by James Boag whose churches were said to resemble granaries. The pulpit installed was in turn transferred to a further "new church" sited there at a later date.

The Rev Mr Sage ruled his congregation with an iron rod. On one occasion, when an elder was brought in front of Session for the third time on a charge of fornication out of wedlock, he was condemned to stand in front of congregation covered in wet sackcloth for the whole of the service!

An interesting fact of the domestic life in the manse was that the minister also held the right of fishing in the River Helmsdale, and a crew of fishers were employed to net the glebe pools. These men also "brewed whisky" for the manse at the annual "brewst" for family use.

Another anecdote was about a colleague, a Rev Mr William Pope minister of Reay, who in 1734 found "a very coarse fellow" occupying a small farm, with a mistress and two children by her. When the culprit failed to appear as required before the Congregation to be rebuked, the Session decided that three strong elders would go to the farm, tie him up with ropes, and then bring him to the service. This they did!

One aspect of religious life which was unusual in the area, involved the participation of laymen on Fridays in the public administration of the Lord's Supper. The ordinance was considered as administered "publicly" when communicants from other parishes joined with those of the parish in its observance, and when on that account there were two distinct services, one in Gaelic and the other in English "with two congregations, the one without, and the other within, doors".

Proceedings began on Thursdays with the "Fast day" when people were encouraged not "to eat or drink unworthily" and to reflect on their past conduct to see if they were worthy to sit at the Lord's Table. This was followed by a similar procedure on Fridays, but, in the north, with the unusual addition of the men "who spoke to the question" i.e. a layman would speak on a verse from the scripture with particular reference to their own lives. The choice of the verse was made by one of the men at the invitation of the minister, and the men who spoke to this verse would, of course, also be put up by the minister. On Saturdays, services were more conciliatory: "Be of good cheer, your sins are forgiven you", Sunday was the great day of the feast and Monday was Thanksgiving Day for blessings enjoyed over the communion season. The Rev Mr Alexander Sage recalled that on one occasion the congregation assembled before the church had numbered between three and four thousand persons.

IV THE CHURCH - POST 1843

To say that 1843 was a watershed year in Scottish religious life is probably to understate the effect of the Disruption that took place within the Established Church of Scotland, and all that followed on from it. Some of the results are still causing problems throughout the country today - a century and a half after the event.

So far as Helmsdale was concerned, either directly or indirectly, it resulted in no fewer than four buildings being constructed by various denominations as churches in which to worship. Today, just as we are about to enter the Millennium only two of these remain in use. One is Bunillidh Church of Scotland, which stands in Castle Park near the entrance to the railway station, and is now the official Parish Church (point 5 in Fig. No. 4), and the other is the Helmsdale Free Church which is not very far from the Bridge Hotel (point 3 on the map in Fig. No. 4). Two former church buildings are now used for secular purposes. One is the former St John's Church (point 2 on the map in Fig. No. 4), and the other the former Free Presbyterian Church (point 4 on the map in Fig. No. 4).

There never has been any Roman Catholic representation, nor, surprisingly, did the Plymouth Brethren make any lasting impact, in spite of the fact that this Brethren movement is so strong on the other side of the Moray Firth. However, in 1886 two Free Church members who had become associated with the Brethren were removed from their former Communion Roll. At the turn of the century, the Brethren had a "Welcome Hall" on the side of the harbour just next to the old Volunteer Drill Hall which had been removed in 1898 when it was required by the adjoining curing yard. By the end of the Second World War, services had ceased to be held in the Welcome Hall, and when the last treasurer, James Ross, Navidale, died in 1960, it was agreed the existing funds could best be used by the Home and Foreign Mission to support Scottish evangelists working in Scotland at locations stretching from Furnace to Tarbolton.

It is not easy to follow all the secessions from the original churches and congregations that took place, so to try and make it as easy to follow as possible, each church will be dealt with separately, beginning with the Church of St John (point 2 on the map in Fig. No. 4). It was formally dedicated in 1841 as the successor of the Church of Kiliain dealt with above, but then only as a Chapel of Ease, since at that time Helmsdale was in the Parish of

Loth where there was still the Parish Church. This anomaly seemed to cause various administrative problems, so in 1846 a petition was lodged with the Court of Teinds by the 2nd Duke of Sutherland asking that the village be transferred to Kildonan Parish. The effect of this Petition, which was granted in January 1847, lasted until the two parishes merged in 1949. Included in the decree making the grant was the provision that the salary of the minister was to be the same as that of the previous minister of Kildonan, (which at that time was vacant) i.e. £150 p.a. plus £8 11s 8d for communion elements, £18 16s 6d in lieu of salmon, and a glebe valued at £30. Later, the payment in lieu of salmon, and the value of the glebe, were to be a constant source of friction between the Rev Mr Scott in Helmsdale and the Sutherland Estates. Between its dedication in 1841, and 1948 when the congregation of Bunillidh Church of Scotland agreed "with reluctance" to join with it, many things happened which were connected with St John's Church.

One of the main things was the 1843 split which affected the whole of the Scottish church, and when in Helmsdale the majority of the congregation left St John's to set up the Helmsdale Free Church it caused a major, lasting division in the whole community. A further lasting division in the Scottish religious scene was created by the uniting in 1900 of the majority of the Free Church of Scotland with the United Presbyterian Church. In Helmsdale, however, a section of the congregation declined to enter the union and remained within the original Free Church.

The relatively few existing records show that in the Parish Church of St John, Mr William Forrest resigned as Session Clerk in 1852 and was replaced by Mr James Campbell the "dominie". At that time, as a result of the 1843 disruption, the Parish Church had 20 communicants (including 2 at the manse) and 17 adherents. The distribution of the communicants was as follows:-

Navidale	2
Helmsdale	12
Gartymore	3
Boghals	1
Manse	2
Total	20

The salary of the new Session Clerk was £3 per annum and from this he had to pay the precentor "as agreed". Usually the precentor, who led the singing of the Psalms, occupied a pulpit, either just below, or to the side of the minister's own pulpit (at that time there were no organs in use). A specimen of this format can be seen in the Timespan Heritage Centre in Helmsdale. The minute of the meeting appointing the new Session Clerk also recorded thanks for the generosity of Loth Church in lending articles for the Sacrament. These were 2 table cloths, 1 bread plate, 1 flagon and 2 communion cups. By 1853 the roll of St John's Parish Church had increased to 74. and in 1857 a new belfry was added. In 1894, the Rev A. B. Scott took over as assistant and successor to the Rev Mr Fraser, and a new era began. He was to hold this charge for over fifty years, almost as long as Mr Campbell, the Session Clerk, who held that position for almost sixty years. Not long after he took up his post, the Rev Mr Scott queried the basis of calculation of his stipend, with particular reference to that part accruing from the salmon fishing. A very acrimonious and inconclusive correspondence on this point, on the upkeep of the walls round the glebe, and its diminishing value brought on by erosion, stretched over about twenty years with Sutherland Estates; in the end, so far as can be gathered, it was to no avail.

When the Rev Mr Scott had taken office the expanding roll caused space at the church to be at a premium, so the Kirk Session passed a resolution that the "Parish Church is unsuitable for public worship, Baptism and the Lord's Supper, largely because of bad position of front gallery". This can be seen from the plan of the church in Fig. No. 6.

Details of the resolution were passed to the Duke of Sutherland, who after some persuasion, and in spite of some acrimonious letters from the Rev Mr Scott, agreed to the alterations, and contributed £120 toward their costs. The renovated and extended Church of St John, with the added luxury of water heating, was reopened for worship by the 4th Duchess of Sutherland two years later in 1896. Concurrent gifts from the congregation included a set of communion plate, a new lectern, a new communion table, a pulpit fall and a reading stool.

St John's Parish Church collections seem very small e.g. in 1904 the annual ordinary collections for the year amounted to £19 3s 1d, (£19.15p) with an amount of £3 12s 4d (£3.62p) for special collections. Fortunately for him, the minister's basic stipend of £150 p.a. was paid by the Heritor, The Duke of Sutherland.

The Sacrament was held regularly - sometimes in private i.e. with only members of the congregation in attendance, but sometimes it was a "public" affair with congregations and ministers from adjacent parishes joining in. These events were more or less week-long celebrations with daily services. During such weeks the school was closed, as the dominie, who was also Session Clerk, was in church. The annual Government grant for schools was partly based on average attendance, so such closures affected the amount payable to the school. Similarly, at these times all boats remained economically unproductive in harbour.

In 1901 a special commemorative Church service was held concurrently with the official funeral service in London of Queen Victoria. To this marched the Volunteers, their arms reversed, under the command of Major Sutherland of Proncy House. Alongside them paraded representatives of the Coastguards and the Naval Reserve. The minister wore black gloves "an old custom of Church of Scotland". His Arts Degree purple hood seemed more appropriate than his white Divinity hood.

The services of a student missionary were obtained for the Kildonan and Kinbrace "outpost" churches soon after Mr Scott came to Helmsdale. This he was only able to arrange after the Kildonan church building was rescued from the farmer in 1894 who had been using it as a store. It had to be substantially renovated. Mr Frank Hardcastle of Suisgill Lodge generously met the costs. Later Miss Radcliffe of Kildonan paid for remounting the bell and providing Bibles and Hymnals for use of the local children. The renovated building was shared by the Rev Mr Grant for Free Church services. Cycling on Sunday was rather frowned upon, but the student missionary at Kildonan required a choir. He recruited the youth from Helmsdale for this purpose. An enthusiastic crew of about twenty cycled the nine miles to Kildonan church (if the weather was fine), although few had any real musical talent. Often they were invited into Kildonan farmhouse for a meal.

The congregation was composed of game keepers, river watchers, farmers, agricultural workers and shepherds. The shepherds were usually accompanied by their dogs, which were left outside the church. Occasionally these dogs attempted to join in the hymns, or sometimes canine jealousies arose leading to open warfare. The shepherds went outside to restore peace, but the language which floated back into the church was colourful and expressive in marked contrast to the preacher.

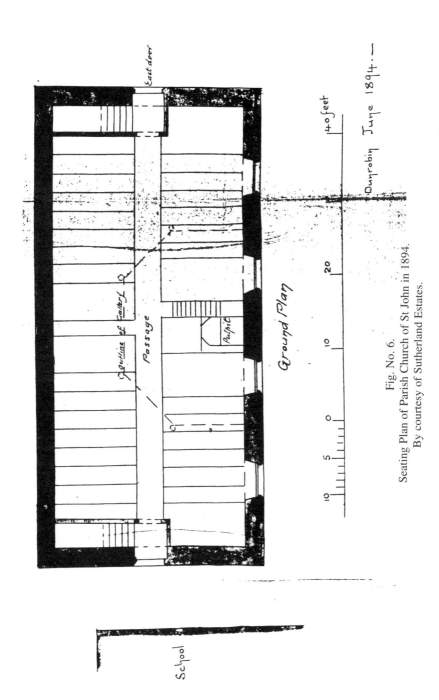

Fig. No. 6.
Seating Plan of Parish Church of St John in 1894.
By courtesy of Sutherland Estates.

Mostly the members of all congregations in the area walked to church, often five or six miles across country. The women folk had a grand time gossiping with each other, both before and after the service. They had little chance of meeting at other times unless they lived in close proximity to some of the estate lodges.

1942 saw the R.A.F leave the manse, part of which they had requisitioned two years earlier, and 1944 was Rev (by now Dr) Scott's jubilee year. After he died on 27th December 1947 the congregation joined with that of Bunillidh Church of Scotland (see below). On his death a most unusual ministry came to an end. He had been in the manse no less than 53 years, for most of which he had been looked after by his sister who survived him. A very studious man, he was greatly concerned with the paucity of enquiry into the Christian missionary work of St Ninian and his associates in Northern Pictland, which had preceded the work of St Columba at Iona. He contributed many learned articles to such publications as The Scottish Historical Review, and the Transactions of the Ecclesiological Society of Scotland, as well as publishing three volumes of his own. Known as "Maister" Scott, he was also diligent in pastoral visitation, even when a boat was required to cross the river to a home. In World War I he had served as chaplain colonel to the 5th Seaforth Highlanders, and brigade chaplain to the Forces.

We turn now to the Helmsdale Free Church. The very handsome building we see today, (point 3 in Fig. No. 4), stands on what was the site of both the original Free Church building and also the Free Church school. As we have seen, the 1843 Disruption affected the whole of the Scottish Church. In Helmsdale, the larger part of the congregation left St John's to set up the Helmsdale Free Church as part of the nationwide Free Church of Scotland. In so doing a major, lasting division in the whole community was created. Initially services were held in fish curing yards in the open. Hugh Miller, in a letter from Cromarty, dated 9th July [1843] observed: "I have just returned from Helmsdale where I have been hearing a sermon in the open air....The congregation was numerous, from six to eight hundred at least...their Gaelic singing... more melancholy than usual...There stretch inland in the background a long, deep, strath...the inhabitants all removed to make way for sheep....the sides of the two hills ...at the sea ...so thickly mottled by little dwellings that it would seem as if the people who had been forced out had struck at its [the sea] mouth. 'We were ruined and made beggars before', they say 'and now they have taken the Gospel from us'. I hear that when the Duke passed through the place, the men stood sulkily looking at him or slunk away into their houses, but that some of the women put out their tongues and began to 'Baa' like sheep."

Very rapidly, however, two somewhat "jerrybuilt" structures were rushed up - one was the Church and the other was the school. The manse followed in 1847, using six building plots originally granted by Duke of Sutherland to Kenneth Sutherland in 1840, but reallocated to the Church.

In 1889, after forty years service, the original Free Church building was in such a bad state of repair that a technical report recommended that "The Church generally is so worn out that.....it would be unwise to attempt to repair it..." Accordingly, both the first Church and schoolroom shown in Fig. No. 5 were demolished and replaced in 1892 by a grand church with 1200 sittings, and a mission hall to hold 300. Together these cost £3,212. This was a large building for the village, but at the time, in addition to the resident congregation there were many visiting herring fishers to be accommodated. It was opened with prayer by Principal Rainy and a photograph of some of those involved in its construction appears in Fig. No. 7.

At the 1900 movement which resulted in the United Free Church, the then minister of the Free Church, the Rev H. Grant, joined the United Free Church, and the vacancy so created was not filled until 1907 because of the litigation over the property titles. It should be explained that prior to this division, the congregation roll amounted to 159 communicants plus 982 adherents, but of these about 130 members, and about 500 adherents, allied themselves with the new United Free Church congregation, leaving only 30 members and 400 adherents with the original Free Church. Since the basis for the allocation of property as established by litigation was that the Free Church retained ownership of property where they held one third of the original worshippers, the Helmsdale church was given to the remaining minority of the original Free Church. This meant the congregation of the new United Free Church of Helmsdale had no property of their own in which to worship.

Fourteen years later, in 1921, the communion roll of this section of the original Free Church still occupying this 1,200-sitting building, was only 6 males and 34 females; the level in 1932 was 7 males and 35 females, and in 1997 average attendances are about 40. In 1929, Mr Mackay, a cabinet maker in Tain, had gifted a new pulpit to the Church; in 1930 the new fishery officer got use of part of Free Church manse; and in 1941 the Church and Mission Hall were requisitioned by army personnel.

Despite changing times, it is well to remember Matthew 18:20 "where two or three are gathered together in my name, there am I in the midst of them".

Next we come to the congregation of United Free Church which in 1900 was made up of the majority of what had been until then, the congregation of the Helmsdale Free Church. As we have seen above there was no Church building immediately available to them, and whilst Kirk Session meetings could be held in school or schoolhouse, something had to be done to provide accommodation in which to worship. In the short term, the congregation had decided this problem was to be resolved by the use of the Drill Hall, but much more satisfactory arrangements were made possible by the very Christian gesture of the Rev Dr Scott and the "moderate" Parish Church Session in allowing the United Free Church the use of their own (St John's) church for their English services at 2 p.m. on Sundays, and in the evenings on alternate Sundays, whilst the Kildonan School Board allowed use of the school for Gaelic services on Sunday afternoons.

These arrangements did not suit all the members of the congregation. Some, although they knew not a word of the Gaelic language, could not bring themselves to enter the 'moderate' kirk, preferring instead to attend the Gaelic service in the school. The national dispute between congregations of the Free Church and congregations of the United Free Church as to who had the legal right to possession of the Free Church buildings took four years to settle and only then could the United Free Church congregation start to build their own place of worship. Consequently, this sharing arrangement with St John's congregation went on for a total of nine years until the new Bunillidh Church in Castle Park was opened for use of the United Free Church congregation in 1909. In 1914 Mrs Rutherford donated two windows to the new church, and in 1916 a bell was hung on the front gable.

The next landmark decision to be taken by the congregation was in 1929, when it was agreed that the United Free Church of Helmsdale was to be known as Bunillidh Church of Scotland. Three years after this, Mrs Rutherford, who had acted as organist for many years without remuneration, retired due to ill health, and, as a mark of appreciation, she was presented

Fig. No. 7.

Some of 1890/92 builders of "new" Helmsdale Free Church. From collection of Helmsdale Heritage Society.

with a Chesterfield sofa and a music cabinet. In 1946 it was agreed that women as elders would not be tolerated; and in 1948 Bunillidh Church of Scotland agreed "with reluctance" to join with St John's Church, with services to be held there, and congregational activities in their own church building. This position continued for a decade when St John's church building and manse were sold, and all Parish religious activity (including the use of the manse for the minister) was moved up to Castle Park.

The last church we have to look at is that used by the Helmsdale Free Presbyterian Church congregation, which came into being in 1893 when another group seceded from the Helmsdale Free Church, and formed the Helmsdale Free Presbyterian Church. For the first thirty-five years of their existence they too had to worship in commercial premises, but a small church was built in Old Caithness Road in 1928 (point 4 on the map in Fig. No. 4). Currently this stands empty. It should perhaps be noted that the congregation merged with that in Halkirk (Caithness) in 1901. Although a small body, its members were sincere, convinced, people. Till the 1980s, a most devoted upholder of the Free Presbyterian principles and the church in Helmsdale was the late William Macintosh, known to all as "Willie Mac" the postmaster, and one of the frequent preachers was the distinguished Rev R R Sinclair of Wick, still very active until his death, aged 98, in 1997.

V CROFTING

The road and bridge works were carried out concurrently with schemes of land development aimed at getting more profit from the land. These involved turning vast areas into sheep farms, and moving out the small cattle-breeder landholders living there. They were driven from their homes to the mouth of the Helmsdale river in the areas known as Navidale, East Helmsdale, Marrel, West Helmsdale and Gartymore. In the original scheme drawn up about 1808, these areas were described as "crofts for fishermen". In retrospect, how sad it is that, in 1799, only a few years previously, from their very meagre resources, these same tenants had managed to contribute £44 16s 6d (£44.85p) to help with the war against France, (say) £20,000 in 1990s terms.

This estate development plan, based on the advice of James Loch, did not turn out as he had forecast. The sheep farms proved unprofitable in the short term: in 1824 the owners were left with Cheviot wool that was "unsaleable in any circumstances". The new holdings for the crofters, averaging three acres, were manifestly insufficient to maintain a family without some additional income. It must be remembered that the potential of the herring fishing was then undeveloped, and what was known of the white fish industry gave no indication it was capable of creating support for all these incoming families. Although conditions improved in 1884 the later clearances, the original terms were that before they moved from their original homes, the last year of their tenure there was rent-free. No other compensation was allowed for improvements made to the land or for the buildings they had left, and the only help that was given toward the construction of new buildings was the provision by the Sutherland Estates of roof framing timbers, and lime. The tenants had to take the building stones off the hill, and provide the thatching. Tenancies could be terminated on four weeks notice and there was no provision for any compensation for improvements made during the tenancies.

The buildings consisted of one room as living accommodation, with separate quarters for livestock which had to be moved down from the previous site. Some idea of the conditions prevailing can be gathered from the exhibit in the Timespan Heritage Centre. To be fair, it must also be pointed out that in 1812-13 and again in 1816-17, when times were really hard and starvation was just round the corner, very large amounts of money and/or meal were distributed by the Sutherland Estates.

In due course, evidence of all this was given to the Napier Commission in 1883, the findings of which resulted in the passing of the 1886 Crofters Holding Act which, amongst other provisions, did away with the practice of immediately doubling the rent to the successor (usually his son), when a crofter died. This iniquitous imposition had been one of the most telling pieces of evidence laid before the hearings of the Napier Commission on Crofting Conditions. Another point which was strongly made was that local roads, as opposed to main roads, were badly maintained.

The same Act also gave crofters substantial security of tenure, and, for the first time, allowed sheep to be kept on the crofts.

Evidence on behalf of Helmsdale crofters on all these matters was given to this Commission by Angus Sutherland (the son of a crofter from West Helmsdale); James Fraser, Crofter, Gartymore; Sinclair Cooper [Couper?], Merchant, Helmsdale; Alexander Gunn, Crofter, Bual, Wester Helmsdale; Adam Bannerman, Crofter, Marrel; George Greig, Auchentoul Lodge; and William MacDonald, Burnside, Navidale.

Brought up in London and in Edinburgh, Countess Elizabeth came to Dunrobin for the first time at the age of about 17. Consequently she had no Gaelic and so, like the other "nobility" of the early 1800s, had no conception of the circumstances of the ordinary man or woman on her estates. The position changed dramatically after the advent of Duchess Millicent in 1884. She was very conscious of what had been done in the name of the family, and went out of her way to try and right some of these wrongs. This she did by forming Highland Home Industries and the Golspie Technical School, both of which measures helped to galvanise the home spinning and woollen industry. She also provided a free medical service for the crofters by launching a branch of Queen Alexandra's Nursing Service. In Staffordshire too, she worked very hard to improve the lot of the workers there, and as a result she earned herself the title of "Meddling Millie"

Those responsible for mismanagement in land development schemes were the factors employed in the early 1800s who lacked the understanding necessary to introduce huge flocks of Cheviot sheep into the hills, moors and glens of the vast Sutherland estate without causing violent upheaval and suffering to the human beings who lived there.

In the undertaking of this task, one individual who was an unmitigated disaster was the evil, infamous, inhuman Patrick Sellar who dealt with the displacement of households under the various "clearance" schemes with a complete lack of human feeling. Between 1810 and 1825 about 9,000 people were moved to the coasts of Sutherland and Caithness. Some problems were to be expected, but nothing could excuse Sellar's complete lack of feeling for his fellow human beings - and yet, not only did the Sutherland Estates continue to pay his annual salary of £250, they also met the defence costs of £621 incurred at his trial for murder arising from the death of an old lady he had evicted. "Damn her, the old witch" he is reported to have said; "she has lived too long, let her burn". At the trial held in Inverness, the jury, composed entirely of local landowners, found him not guilty of the charge. He was allowed to keep his job, but the Sheriff-Substitute, Robert McKidd, who had brought the charge, was not so fortunate. He was dismissed.

William Young was initially engaged in a consultative capacity, because he had experience on his own small estate but turned out to be a visionary without much idea of how to exercise the financial control required by these major developments instigated by Lord Stafford, later to become the 1st Duke of Sutherland.

Whilst there were earlier displacements, the move down into the crofts round Helmsdale probably started around 1812. Under Mr Francis Suther, who had previous experience on the Stafford estate at Trentham, these moves were carried out with more humanity. Those moving down from Strathnaver were starting to make preparation at their new crofts at Helmsdale in 1819 and then completed the move into "larger houses with pigs outside the living accommodation and the cattle in a separate building" in 1820.

Fuel was mainly peat and each croft was allowed its own peat bank, mostly well out in the hills. The peats were cut, dried, stacked and conveyed home as circumstances permitted. Those who had not a pony or horse had to borrow from a neighbour and, as cash was a scarce commodity, the loan was repaid with labour, such as helping the neighbour with his peats, or his harvesting.

Some idea of the style of agriculture carried on by the crofters can be gathered from the details of crops grown and livestock shown in Tables A, B, C, and D. In interpreting these, however, it must be borne in mind that the data shown also includes that of the farms owned by the Estate, so with separate acreages for farms and crofts not available, detailed comparisons are not possible. What is interesting, however, is the comparison of the 188 crofts in Kildonan in 1895 (see Table A) as against the 140 under cultivation

41

today as shown in the Statistical Account for 1984 - and of the latter, many are sublet or let for grazing.

No details are available of the type of agriculture adopted by the small landholders before the clearances were implemented, but a picture of what it was like can be gathered from the comments contained in Donald Macleod's "Gloomy Memories".

"Down to the period at which the calamities accompanying the CLEARING system overtook us, and before we came under the LOCH [name of factor] iron rod... we lived ...a happy life.... Some years our corn crops would fail but we had cattle which we could sell, and purchase food with the price of them; we had sheep and goats which we could take and eat; we had salmon and trout for the taking; we had abundance of milk, butter and cheese; and none of us ever died of famine".

By way of contrast a rather more detailed description of 19th century croft life has been pieced together from some local archive material, which also helps the understanding of the bald statistics in the tables.

The crops were mainly oats, barley, potatoes and turnips. Cereal and hay crops were cut by the scythe and sometimes with a sickle. The oats were thrashed by the flail, and the grain taken to the mill. The precious oatmeal, stored in meal chests or meal barrels usually made by coopers at the harbour, kept well and was the mainstay of the family throughout the winter. Sowans (husks) were also retained, steeped in water overnight and made into a thick gruel which was easily digested.

'Sea-weed' was greatly used as manure and 'night soil' was preserved for a like purpose.

Chaff was used to fill the ticking for beds and was renewed yearly. This was supposed to be sleep-inducing and very healthy.

Straw was used to feed animals, sometimes with the addition of a little diluted treacle. It was also used as bedding for the animals, and along with heather and turf, to re-thatch roofs of houses and steadings.

Later, the whins introduced to vary animal feeding were browsed by the sheep, which seemed to enjoy cropping closely the bushes on the 'whinny knowe'.

Most crofters had grazing rights on the hills for their animals. The numbers allowed to graze were calculated by reference to the size of the crofts.

Heather and willow were used to make the sweeping brooms, (besoms), pot scrubbers and baskets. These were often sold round the doors by the 'tinkers', along with pots, pans, horn and bone spoons. The latter had the great advantage that they did not absorb heat and so did not burn one's mouth.

Drinking water was procured from wells and had to be carried in pails supported by yokes or girds (a form of belt). In many cases water had also to be carried for the animals. Incredible as it may seem, some crofts had electricity before they had running water laid on by the local authority.

Incidentally, piping water into houses put an end to the old tradition of the housewives queuing up at the well, so that the first could get the "good luck" pail of the New Year, immediately after midnight.

Washing of clothes and household items was usually done near the well or burn - fires were lit, wooden tubs filled, and the scrubbing boards were vigorously used. Blankets were 'tramped' by foot in early summer. On fine days, every one seemed to be busy cleaning the winter's soiled linen and bedding, and drying and bleaching items in the sun.

The women knitted all the woollen garments, such as vests, long johns, socks, and sweaters with fancy patterns, as well as stockings from oiled wool for the sea boots.

After the change in the crofters holdings legislation, sheep were allowed along with cattle, and poultry; and most crofters, as well as many of the fisher folk, kept pigs, which were smoked, cured, pickled and stored against the winter. The open peat hearths and access to the wide (often "hanging lum") chimneys afforded an easy means of smoking bacon and hams.

In some cases local wool was washed, spun and woven in the crofts. Up to about 1880 large quantities were shipped to brokers in Leith, but with the coming of the railways things began to change. Firstly, ever-increasing quantities were sent for spinning and weaving both to the mill in Brora as well as to MacNaughtons in Pitlochry. Initially the former was run by a Yorkshire firm but was taken over by Mr T M Hunter in 1901. Later, large quantities were sent to wool brokers in Glasgow whose principals were carpet factories there. This in turn resulted in the 4th Duke and Duchess Millicent sponsoring the setting up of three carpet factories, one of which was in Helmsdale, another in Embo where it operated under the control of the local dominie, Mr Phimister; and one in Lybster. After about two years the management passed into the control of Templetons of Glasgow who only ran them for about a further two years, as they closed in 1908.

In the year before Duchess Millicent passed control of the carpet factory to Templetons of Glasgow, a Helmsdale made carpet had been on show in the premises of Messrs Warings, of Oxford Street, London, who "had opened an agency to take orders". At the time of the takeover she had entertained "her girls" to tea in the "Welcome Hall" which was almost next door to the factory. This entertainment included songs by Lieut. Egerton from Navidale (of "Gem" rescue fame), the quartet "Nobleman and Beggars", and also from some of the carpet makers themselves.

In the 19th century barter also prevailed, when on Saturdays the crofters' wives took their eggs and butter to the local shops and exchanged them for groceries and often an ounce of bogie roll and/or a clay pipe for their menfolk. Many of the latter used flints and steels instead of matches to procure a light.

Fish of all sorts were pickled by the householders and one might get salmon, trout and sea trout as well as the ordinary white fish when one dipped into a barrel.

Rabbits were never a menace in crofting areas.

Venison and mutton were pickled and smoked. The venison was often illegally acquired, but the skins were also preserved. It was common to see a deer skin which had been split across the middle. This had been done to enable a half stag, or more probably a hind, to be carried home across the poachers' shoulders.

Poaching was commonplace among the crofts which bordered the hills and, more often than not, was winked at as long as it was only for home-consumption. Today little has changed. Not so long ago kind-hearted salmon poachers shared their spoils with elderly residents in Helmsdale. One pensioner had trouble with her conscience so she went and asked the local constable what she should do with it. With a deadpan face the officer replied "Poach it".

The late Miss Margaret Sutherland, Navidale, took a more pragmatic view, and expressed her pleasure by recording it in the following poem:-

Robin Hood and his men emerged from the wood,
To give the pensioners a taste of the rich man's food.
It was salmon poached from Prince Charlie's beat,
So the poachers delivered a right royal treat.
It was neatly parcelled and pinned to each door,
But removing the pin was a bit of a chore.
One worried recipient reported the matter,
And the bobby's advice was -"Put it in water".
While the salmon was sizzling in fries, roasts and stews,
The press had a field day reporting the news.
At least it was good news to give us some cheer -
A change from the scandal and gloom that we hear.
So thanks to the poachers for raising a laugh,
If only the salmon hadn't suffered the gaffe.

Interestingly, today, almost two centuries on, the original layout of West Helmsdale crofts, can be seen from the Telford Bridge, almost completely unaltered except from the great improvement in the standard of the houses.

VI COMMERCIAL FISHING

The earliest reference to commercial fishing is found when we read in the local guidebook produced by "Timespan", of salted, as well as boiled and pickled (in vinegar) salmon, being exported as far as Bordeaux in 1740.

Around this time the market for salmon in London was growing rapidly, and, to a large extent, was being supplied from Berwick-upon-Tweed, where, at times, some 60,000 stones of salmon were being taken from the river annually, an extraction rate that could not continue indefinitely. Interestingly, from 1788 the fish were preserved in ice for shipment, and by 1799 7,600 carts of ice were being used annually, but this practice was only adopted in Helmsdale for herring about 1840.

A rising demand for salmon from the various markets had to be met from somewhere, and Helmsdale became one of the sources targeted. In consequence the facilities were upgraded, and by 1791 we find a new salmon boiling house had been "lately erected", and by 1810 the salmon fishing is described as "pretty successful at present. Cruives [wattled fish traps] and dykes are in excellent order. Fish are boiled, salted or pickled, packed in boxes or in Kitts [small barrels] and sent to Aberdeen by a small vessel belonging to the company [Berwick on Tweed Salmon Fisheries Company], from where they are reshipped to London by smack".

The then lessees, Messrs Landles and Redpath, had come originally from Berwick-upon-Tweed, where they were master coopers, and were part of the Berwick Salmon Fisheries Company, but they had other Helmsdale interests because they are shown as tenants of "Dry Multures of Gartymore and Milne" in East Helmsdale.

Salmon fishings of Naver, Torrisdale, Helmsdale and Brora were let to a consortium of the said James Landles and Philip Redpath of Berwick on Tweed, with George Riddle, also of Berwick on Tweed, Henry Morton of Berrington, County Durham, George Redpath and William Redpath fishmongers in Billingsgate as cautioners (guarantors). The annual rent in 1808 was £2,267 but by 1815 it dropped to £1,605. In addition to the rent the "family" was entitled to 100 fish each year free of charge.

Apparently the dykes and cruives were not altogether satisfactory, because by 1829 stake nets were being recommended for use at the mouth of the harbour.

Herring soon superseded the trapping of the salmon, and to understand how this came about we have to go back in history. When, for no known reason, the herring shoals forsook the Baltic in the early 1500s, the Dutch were quick to seize their opportunity, and by 1600 their herring fleet numbered about 1,500. By the middle of the 18th century, however, their economy had become affected by their many wars and they began to lose their market share. This allowed Wick, which up to then had been mostly line-fishing for white fish, and then Helmsdale, to break into Continental markets.

White fish were usually caught using lines with baited hooks a method completely different from that used to catching herring. This was done using drift nets which were shot at dusk and when hauled at dawn, the catch was shaken out into the hold.

At first nets were made of hemp, hand-spun, twisted into twine, and made into narrow lengths called "lints". These were laced together, one below the other, and tanned to preserve them. This was usually done in a solution made from the bark of oak or ash trees. In the 1850s, these were superseded by cotton nets, woven on a loom invented by James Paterson of Musselburgh.

At the start of each season nets and lines had to be 'barked', with corks and floats attached carefully so that they ran out freely.

At the height of the herring season the men would only spend two nights in bed each week - on the other nights, if their boats had no decking, they had only the sail for cover.

When the Helmsdale herring fishing was on, boats came from all around the coast and it was said that one could walk across the river on the decks of the boats. Some indication of this can be gathered from Fig 8.

Many trades were engaged in keeping boats seaworthy. Small boys particularly loved to watch and see if the shipwrights who worked with adzes, would cut the toe of their boots - which they never did - and to see them caulking was a treat in itself.

At the quayside, catches of herring were unloaded by round baskets into long, shallow wooden troughs about four feet wide, where a sprinkling of salt enabled the grippers to hold the slippery fish to gut them. The round baskets held a quarter of a cran.

Behind each girl employed to gut there would be three shallow tubs into which the gutted fish were thrown according to size and quality. From there the packer would take an armful, drop the herring into the barrel and

Fig. No. 8.
Harbour crowded with boats c.1880. From collection of John Sutherland.

48

pack them in layers, bellies up, and separated by a layer of salt just coarse enough to keep the fish from touching each other, but hard enough to withstand pressure.

Each barrel held between 750 and 1,000 fish depending on size and quality, and all salt used was imported either from France or Spain as Scottish salt was not considered suitable. In the early years (although the practice was relaxed later), before being exposed for sale, each barrel was checked both by an intending purchaser and an inspector, and was then branded as proof of its contents. The extent of the relaxation was quite substantial as only one barrel in ten had to be inspected.

So rapid was the rate of improvement in the catches made, that 20,060 barrels of herring were noted in 1819, the same year as upwards of 5,246 registered tons of shipping were cleared. Just what this meant to the harbour are can be gathered from the famous painting by Daniell reproduced in Fig. 9.

As will be seen from Table G, the most productive year for Helmsdale seems to have been 1841 when 39,504 barrels were caught. However disastrous years followed in 1869, 1870, 1871, and 1878.

To get some indication as to the extent of the total trade shared between Helmsdale and Wick, it is worth recalling that in 1862, one thousand and twenty two boats fished out of Wick during the six weeks season, and about two hundred and fifty from Helmsdale. Whisky flowed like water. Upwards of 500 gallons a day were consumed in Wick alone, where 22 public houses, and 23 across the river in Pulteney, supplied the needs of the thousands who looked to the herring to supply their livelihood for the rest of the year. Against this background it is understandable that an attempt was made to start a distillery in Helmsdale.

Prior to the introduction of seine netting for white fish in 1928, fishermen's wives had a very hard life indeed. Without a good wife a fisherman could hardly have been expected to ply his calling, so most tended to marry young. The women had to 'redd' the great lines, rebait them, and arrange the line properly in the skeps or line boxes, so that they ran freely when 'shot' at sea. Boys had to bring up the mussels in a barrow and open them ready for the women to use, and were also expected to "redd" the lines. If within the family no reward was forthcoming, doing someone else's line usually earned a 6d.

Nor was that all. During the rest of the day, besides looking after the

49

Fig. No. 9.
Picture of Harbour c. 1820.   From Painting by Daniell.

50

family, wives often peddled their creels round the crofts and houses, knitting as they went, Shetland fashion, with one of their needles fixed to their belt. The fisher women employed in the yards as gutters, worked at speeds which were almost incredible. They also followed the fish and so usually finished the season at Yarmouth. Usually their accommodation was in barracks or odd rooms. Frequently, when there was too much work for the Helmsdale girls to cope with, "outsider" girls from Brora and Embo were brought in. These ordinarily got a retainer of about £2 at the start of each season.

Although physically less arduous for the women, the 1930s saw things again very hard because of the depressed state of the fishing. Being self-employed, fisherfolk were not eligible for unemployment relief. One fisherman recalled that for a time his mother's weekly housekeeping allowance was 14/-. Even at that time this could not feed the family, so at least two of the local merchants Messrs Rapson and Messrs Traill introduced a system of credit books, into which essentials could be charged for payment as and when possible. Happily they were never let down.

At this time most of the boats were rudimentary, open-decked "scaffies" able to be pulled up on shore, but the stronger covered-decked "fifies" were also starting to make their appearance. It was 1880 before the more elegant "Zulu" boats appeared.

A boat-building yard was started in 1908, but does not seem to have stayed in business for very long.

Small children used to enjoy watching the boats set sail - for the very selfish reason that crews were inclined to fling ship's biscuits (like square dog biscuits) to them as they left the harbour.

Before fish auctions commenced at Wick and elsewhere in 1905, boats were often "thirled" to one of the local curers for each season, on an agreement which included a set price for the fish landed and also might guarantee a dram for each man.

This type of arrangement is reflected in the terms of a lease James Methven took of a plot to southeast of Castle Park. The tack duty was £3 per annum, and part of the agreement was he had to build a fish curing shed to value of £500 and a dwelling to value of £10.

As further dues, he had to pay:-

For each boat belonging or engaged to him 2/6d per season, plus 3d for each time it entered port, and for each barrel of herring he cured - a half penny.

In 1864 the curers working, and number of boats affiliated to them, were:-

James Matheson	69
David Davidson	16
Robt Fraser Jr.	6
William Gow	33
George Couper	20
Peter Sutherland	14
John McLeod	63
Donald Couper	14
Donald Fraser	26
John Ross	3
	264

William Bruce)
Robt Fraser Sr.)   chance boats.

Typical terms of engagement for each boat included a "start" payment of £5, a bottle of whisky per boat per week, and a daily dram for each member of the crew.

In fishing, death is never far away, and one of the worst disasters that struck the community was on 18th August 1848, when, of the 130 boats which put to sea from Helmsdale, two were upset at the bar, two floundered at sea, and one was wrecked at the entrance to the harbour. The total loss of life was 13 men. At Wick on the same night, of the approximate number of 800 boats that put to sea, fifty-three boats were lost.

The curers yards employed men all the year round making barrels which were stocked against the herring season. The coopers started work in the very early morning and the yards were lit up with the fires which were used in their trade. Most of the coopers were also crofters and when their day finished in the yards, they went home to their crofts. They were better paid than the average tradesman.

Today coopers are rarely found working outside the whisky distilleries, but a century ago it was reckoned they made up about 5% of all tradesmen. This is not surprising when it is borne in mind that then there were no plastic containers, and every housewife needed something to hold her vegetables, her flour, her meal, her salt, and all other household stores, In addition she needed such items as washtubs, butter churns and other similar items.

A cooper's standard of skill had to be such that he could construct a barrel or cask from start to finish without using gauge or rule, and the finished article had to be capable of keeping the pickle in, the weather out, and withstanding the rough usage to which a full barrel must necessarily be subjected. At the end of his apprenticeship he had to produce an "apprentice piece" to the satisfaction of his master. One such piece, in the form of a flask and drinking vessel, is reproduced in Fig. 10, and may be seen in the Timespan Heritage Centre .

Today whisky barrels are all of oak, but the herring barrels were made of spruce brought over from Scandinavia if no home grown supplies such as birch, which came from the west coast, were available.

As will be gathered from the large variations in the numbers of barrels exported each year as shown in Tables F and J (which would also reflect on the amounts of salt needed), making arrangements for the necessary funds to carry on the business would be very difficult indeed. At times it would put a very considerable strain on the finances of the curers: there is evidence of "mortgaging to the hilt" and the obtaining of personal guarantees to meet the requirements of the bank. The prudence of such measures became all too clear after the disastrous seasons around 1888, when the North of Scotland Bank Ltd (known as the curers bank) had to write off advances amounting to something like, in 1990 terms, £10 million.

Local coopering was discontinued temporarily in 1914 and permanently in 1939. Many barrels were then brought in by ship. Fig No. 11 shows a Couper-owned boat (S.S. Berridale) loaded with such a cargo.

At the most, herring fishing only lasted about five months in the year, and (before the days of seine netting) for the rest of the time the boats went for white fishing with hand lines, either hooks with bait, or a ripper - a lump of lead (cylindrical with hooks attached). The latter was drawn up and down on a line, and caught mostly cod which were deceived by the gleaming lead cylinder.

Crab and lobster fishing was also carried out as it is today, with creels set amongst the rocks.

The material used to make sea boots was stiff, which made them very difficult to remove, so each fisherman carried a very sharp knife in his right trouser pocket so that, in the case of an emergency, he could cut his boots off quickly. On the other hand many adopted the opposite policy of not learning to swim, so that any accidental live immersion in water would not be prolonged.

Oilskins were usually made by the men themselves. Strong cloth was shaped into jackets or trousers, and then treated with repeated applications of linseed oil.

For those interested in the local timetable of the growth of the herring trade, the development seems to have started in Brora in 1811 where houses for fishers from Aberdeenshire and Fife were built. Coincidentally, when the war with Napoleon was over, a Dutch prisoner of war decided to stay on in Scotland and marry a Portgower girl, so the residents there were amongst the first to learn Dutch secrets of preserving fish.

Some three years later, in 1814, the only boats based on Helmsdale were those connected with salmon fishing, but that position changed rapidly with the introduction of a Government bounty of 4/- per barrel on herring caught by small boats.

A salt cellar and a cooper's shop were constructed at a cost of £77 15s 10d; Messrs A. & D. Simpson from Morayshire got an advance of £1,200 @ 6.5% to build a curing yard and sheds; Messrs Landles and Calder got an advance of £2,200 to build a larger yard and red herring house; curing yards were also built by Messrs Bell of Leven, Redpath of Berwick, Miller Robertson and Nelson of Leith, Ross of Golspie, and Messrs Simpsons; and Mr D Horne erected a shed for wool storage. The exact location of most of these yards can be identified in the street map shown in Fig. No. 1.

Work on a pier and breastworks for the harbour commenced in 1816, the same year as the first Fishery Officer was stationed at Helmsdale. The pier was completed two years later.

Just how rapidly the herring trade built up can be gathered from the following five year statistics:-

	Coopers	Women	Men	Boats	Barrels
1814	8	60	80	20	2,400
1815	17	130	200	50	4,000
1816	32	240	400	80	7,300
1817	44	330	550	110	9,350
1818	70	520	700	140	14,390
1819	70	645	1,020	204	20,060

As we can see from Table G, catches, broadly speaking, remained at the 20,000 barrel level until 1837 when they increased considerably, although there were less than successful years in 1821, 1832 and 1834.

Fig. No. 10.
Cooper 'Prentice Piece of
Wooden Flask with Stopper, and Tumbler,
and last remaining Helmsdale-distilled whisky.
By Courtesy of Late J D Campbell.

Fig. No. 11.
S. S. Berridale loaded with barrels (c.1925). By Courtesy of Mrs Catherine Burns, Inverness.

The nature of coastwise (as opposed to foreign) traffic that came into the harbour, and is not included in the Tables E, F, H and J, is also very interesting. From Inverness came stave wood; from Leith, Liverpool, and to a lesser extent, Wick came salt; other items came from London, Perth, Thurso, Montrose, Berwick, Newcastle, Banff, Kirkcaldy, Dunbar, and Sunderland.

Foreign exports went to places like Belfast, Elsinore, Norway, Hamburg, Stettin, and Riga, with imports coming, for example, from Danzig (Deal ends); and from Bremen (salt, and empty barrels). In the circumstances it is not surprising to find a house had been rented to a tidewaiter (Customs Officer) by 1820 and its location beside the harbour can still be identified by the name and the Sutherland Coat of Arms on the wall.

No doubt influenced by the growth in trade, the Sutherland Estates in 1828 promoted a private Act of Parliament for repair, maintenance and government of harbour. Perhaps not wholly coincidentally, the next year saw the firm of George Couper & Co. starting to trade by importing barrels of salt from Spain, as well as barrels of tar from Archangel.

Around this time ice was becoming a popular medium for fish preservation, so an ice-house and pond were built about 1840. At broadly the same time, a steam sawmill was brought in to help the coopers. This did not meet with everyone's approval, as it had to be fired up very early each morning, rather to the annoyance of close neighbours.

Although partially offset by the availability of work on the railway, 1869 and 1870 were bad herring seasons and saw "Destitution in parish". 1871 was little better as, whilst the number of summer herring boats was 250 (33 more than 1870), catches were 52 crans per boat as against 72 in 1870. Other disastrous year were 1878 which saw catches drop by almost 90%, and 1880 when results were similar.

The village was honoured by a VIP visit when, in 1882, the Duke of Edinburgh visited the newly-completed Coastguard Station.

In spite of these disastrous years, things did improve eventually, and seven years later, the ever-increasing volume of trade made it imperative that a larger harbour be provided as a matter of some urgency. So that the benefit of Public Loan Board funding could be obtained, a Provisional Committee for Harbour Trustees was established. This included the 3rd Duke of Sutherland, Mr George Gunn, his factor, Rev W. Fraser, Mr George Hill, and Mr James Campbell. Plans for a new harbour were approved, a new dredger to cost £2,200 was ordered, and in the following year (1890) the Helmsdale Harbour Order came into force. In essence, under the terms of this, the harbour was gifted to the Harbour Trustees, who were Duke of Sutherland, the Marquess of Stafford; Donald Maclean, factor, Rhives; Rev John Murray, Brora, County Convenor; John Gunn, George Couper, James Burns Fraser, William Cuthbert and John MacAulay all fishcurers; George Ross, hotelkeeper; James John Hill, Bank Agent; William McAngus, fisherman; James Campbell, Inspector of the Poor; James Paterson, merchant and postmaster; and Rev Daniel Fraser.

Whilst it was estimated the cost of the new harbour would be £16,630 made up of:-

Sea Wall	£ 4,897
New Quay	5,945
Jetty	1,503
Groyne	2,305
Excavations	1,980
	£16,630
in fact the actual cost was	£13,814

In line with this expansion, the old distillery buildings were converted from a hospital into fishermen's cottages. These were to be rented out at £1 15/- per half year for a dwelling, or if for the storage of barrels at ½d per barrel. In one season George Couper was storing 1,020 barrels.

In the next year (1892) the Harbour Extension Foundation Stone was laid by the 3rd Duchess of Sutherland and a bottle was buried under it containing a 5/- piece, copies of local newspapers, and the Harbour Act Loan Document. The layout of the harbour included provision for a breakwater, which, a few years later, had to be opened up to allow salmon to have access upstream. This is known as Hardy's Hole and is named after the only fisherman prepared to come through it into the harbour on a regular basis. As usual in the village "Hardy" is a nickname - in this case for Johnnie and his brother, the late George Sutherland.

In celebration of the laying of the stone, a Cake and Wine Banquet was held in the Drill Hall, and workmen got lunch in Ross's hotel at 1/6d each. Naturally the Volunteers had to provide a Guard of Honour. A copy of the formal toast list for this is shown in Fig. No. 12. It would appear the economics of running the harbour were at times rather less than satisfactory. In 1912 the Couper family were paying a rent for it, providing the managerial services for it without charge, and still making a loss on it.

In the last years of the century, steam drifters began to appear. By 1905, the Couper family owned eleven of them. These seem to have been held either by individual members of the family, through the medium of one of their associated companies, or, in at least one case, in partnership with another individual. The companies in question were the Strath Steamship Co. Ltd, Helmsdale or Messrs Downing, (otherwise known as Downing and Sutherland), Cardiff, whilst the only individual partner known was a Mr George T Grey.

The method of profit sharing adopted in the latter case was that after meeting running costs, the remaining surplus (or deficit) was shared equally between the crew, the owners of the boats, and the owners of the nets. Around 1912 the profit margins seem to have provided a very inadequate return on the capital employed.

In 1905, these drifters (and the skippers where these were known) were as follows:-

Ada (Thomas MacKay, Helmsdale), Bertha (John MacKay, Helmsdale), Bluebell (Donald Bremner, Wick), Clara, (James McCrae, Brora), Dora (Alex McAngus, Helmsdale), Ella (Alex Moir, Macduff), Flora (James Innis, Helmsdale), Margaret, Pansy (William Flett, Findochty), Primrose (James Moir, Wick), Sylfaen, (skipper not known).

As the name of the last vessel is Welsh and translates as ""foundation" one wonders if it was used around Cardiff. It is also interesting to note that by 1912 it had been replaced by the cargo vessel "Watchful", and six of the vessels, although still apparently under the Couper name, were part owned by Mr George T Grey.

In the "off season" many of these boats lay in the Inner Harbour, and, for their safety, as we have seen, a boom was constructed in 1907.

Later cargo vessels owned within the Couper family included SS "Helmsmuir", "Linus", "Watchful", "Hessle", "Berridale", "Halladale", "Portaferry" and "Helmsdale"".

Advice from the Royal National Lifeboat Institution as to the type of boat most suited to the village was rejected, and another type costing £380 was established in the village in 1908. The boat was named "Cobhar nan Mharich" (The Mariners Help) and was transported free of charge from

HELMSDALE HARBOUR.

Laying of Foundation Stone

BY

Her Grace The Duchess of Sutherland.

BANQUET IN ARTILLERY HALL,

on

Saturday, 20th August, 1892, at 2 o'clock p.m.

Chairman, - - DONALD M'LEAN, Esq.,

CHAIRMAN OF HARBOUR TRUST.

TOAST LIST

"The Queen," ... ... THE CHAIRMAN.

"The Prince and Princess of Wales and }
other Members of the Royal Family," } THE CHAIRMAN.

"The Duke and Duchess of Sutherland," Rev. DANIEL FRASER, M.A.

NOTE.—The Rev. Mr. Fraser will, on behalf of the Fishermen and others, present
His Grace with an Address.
REPLY BY THE DUKE.

"Success to the Harbour," ... ... MAJOR HILL.
REPLY BY JOHN GUNN, ESQ. OF ALDIE.

"The Town and Trade of Helmsdale," ... Rev. A. GRANT.
REPLY BY JAMES PATERSON, ESQ.

"The Engineer," ... ... GEORGE COUPER, Esq.
REPLY BY MR. BARRON, C.E.

"Strangers," ... ... J. J. HILL, Esq.

"The Chairman," ... ... JAMES CAMPBELL, Esq.

J. RUSSELL, PRINTER, ABERDEEN.

Fig. No. 12.
Toast List for Banquet in Artillery Hall
on Laying of Harbour Foundation Stone (1892).
By Courtesy of Sutherland Estates.

60

London on the Couper vessel "Watchful". Because their advice was rejected, no financial help was available from the Institution, so all monies had to be raised locally. This was soon available and included contributions from Mr Andrew Carnegie, the Dukes of Sutherland and Portland, and local residents.

By 1913 it was found necessary to ask for subscriptions to maintain the lifeboat. The rate was fixed at £1 10/- per motor boat, and in 1922 each fisherman over 16 was required to give 2/- annually. Later monies were raised by boats donating select boxes of haddock for sale at the market. Before the station closed in 1939 rescues effected included the "Gem" 1912, "St Abbs" and "Ivy" in 1923, and finally "Geary" in 1925. Various rewards for these rescues were paid by the R.N.L.I., and for their part in the "Gem" rescue, silver medals for bravery and thanks in vellum were presented to Alexander Main (Jr) and Lieut Egerton. Nowadays R.N.L.I. cover is available from Wick.

By the end of the First World War motor driven fishing boats were starting to appear and then in 1921 Arthur Cadogan Vachell bought Helmsdale harbour and ice-house. Unfortunately Mr Vachell got into financial difficulties, and the Harbour passed to the Official Receiver, Cardiff. Luckily, the position was saved, mainly by the Couper family who provided most of the necessary funds required to buy out the Official Receiver's interest. In 1933 the property in the harbour passed to Sutherland County Council, who became responsible for its operation. This is now done by means of a Local Authority committee.

In 1975, the last year of the old County of Sutherland, running costs for the harbour were £12,014 as against revenue of £872 - a rate-borne cost of £11,142 for the year, whilst capital expenditure by the County Council from 1933 to that date was £158,096, and there was little chance of its being recovered from harbour revenue.

A coastguard station was established in 1882. Then it was manned by two full-time coastguards, backed up by local volunteers. By 1951 the local fleet was down to 11 seine net vessels and 6 lobster boats, so its status was reduced, and watch was kept by local men on a "bad weather" watch basis.

At the same time six men were employed by the estates in the Kildonan Strath on salmon netting in the season.

VII SHOOTING AND FISHING

One source of revenue to the community in the late 19th century was the escalation of "hunting, shooting and fishing" for sport. Unfortunately none of the very early game records of the lodges has survived, so no details of early bags are available. People of substance, arriving on the trains from London, were met by the shooting brakes from the lodges when the season opened. The local stores were called on frequently for luxury goods to meet the "necessities" for this clientele. No visit to the village would have been complete without buying a pair of Walter Davidson's marvellous handmade boots or shoes. His scale of charging seemed to vary according to whether the purchaser was a native or not.

Tweed and woollen goods were in demand, and the spoils of the sport had to be packaged for the sportsman to carry home.

In 1952 the sporting estates and owners were:-

Baddanloch	George I Wood
Auchentoul	Sir Harold Nutting
Borrobol	Sir Roderick Wigan
Suisgill	Lady Paynter
Torrish	McCorquodale family.

There was also the Lodge of Salzcraggie which had sixty rooms but it was demolished in 1950.

By 1888, as it is today, fishing rights in the private section of the River Helmsdale were divided into twelve beats containing 178 pools. In the original pamphlet these were described as:-

I Lower Beats

1. From   the sea to head of Craggie Pool.
2. From   Craggie to the tail of Lower Torrish pool.
3.   "   Lower Torrish to the tail of Baddywood pool.
4.   "   Baddywood to top of Kilcar Dyke pool.
5.   "   Kilcar Dyke pool to top of Kildonan Dyke pool.
6.   "   Kildonan Dyke pool to Kildonan Bridge.

II Upper Beats

1. Kildonan Bridge to parapet below Suisgill Lodge.
2. From   said parapet to foot of island above surfaceman's
   house.
3. "   said Island to Kinbrace Railway Bridge
4. "   said Bridge to Junction of Baddanloch Water.
5. "   said Junction to Loch-Namoine.
6. To be Loch-Namoine.

The detailed format today is rather different, but still consists of twelve beats, six above, and six below Kildonan Bridge. Originally the pool above Kildonan Bridge was known as the Bridge Pool, but this was renamed the "Poor Lady Pool" after a tragedy on 19th June 1927 when Mrs Margery Eadon was accidentally drowned whilst fishing there. Her husband was fishing in the pool on the down side of the bridge, and was alerted to the tragedy when her hat came floating down on the current.

To ensure a stable level of water for fishing a dam was constructed at Loch Baddanloch in 1902 and rebuilt 70 years later.

The level of catches has varied immensely from year to year, but it is understood in the years 1975 to 1979 the number of salmon and grilse caught was as follows:

1975	2395
1976	1578
1977	2188
1978	2546
1979	2734

The most productive months seem to have been July and September. It is probably worth bearing in mind that no figures are available for catches on the tidal, public water, and the practice of netting at the river mouth ceased in the early 1980s.

In spite of the lack of official records some tales have come down to us.

For example, at one of the shooting lodges a keeper was requested to keep the household supplied with salmon. The river was very low at one period and he procured the fish by shooting them as they attempted to leap up the falls. Very unfortunately for him, one of these was found to contain some shot pellets - the cause was investigated and Bobby got the 'sack'.

The lessee of one lodge was Miss Radcliffe, a lady who personally had no interest in sport but kept renting the place as a tradition, because her father, a keen sportsman, had done so for many years.

She always had the lodge filled with invited guests - some wealthy and some not. At the end of one season, she was consoling a keen but impecunious sportsman on the poor bags he had had. He replied that he was very well-satisfied as he could not afford to give big tips to the staff who reserved privileged positions on the shoot for wealthy guests giving good tips.

Miss Radcliffe was furious, summoned all the outdoor staff and informed them that the people who could not afford to give big tips were to get priority over her wealthy guests, and were to get the opportunity of obtaining the biggest bags. If they were not proficient shots, they must be assisted. If her orders were not complied with, there would be changes in staff.

Lodges were somewhat spartan affairs till the ladies started to accompany the sportsmen and demanded some comfort and modern conveniences, and ultimately luxury accommodation.

Dogs were trained and retained by the keepers - the hiring of dogs came much later. Some of the estates became famous for their dogs and their training skills.

Trappers were the only people who really sold their catches to the markets - game, venison, and hares were much more often distributed or sold locally. Many of the keepers graduated from poaching families (the saying was that the best keeper was an ex-poacher).

It was not only incomers who enjoyed field sports. No permit was needed to catch brown trout in the tidal waters at the river mouth, and of course any salmon caught there by accident were always put back! The local bank managers, the dominie and others had permits to fish and shoot when required. In the closed season such gentlemen spent at least part of their time in dressing flies, pleating lines with horse hair, renewing landing nets, checking reels, guns and the other paraphernalia. On occasion the help of an expert was sought. In more recent times, Miss Megan Boyd of Kintradwell, whose skill in tying flies for the "gentry", including Prince Charles, was well known, came into this category.

Sometimes legal fishing could be infuriating. Once, when one of the local permit holders had fished the Marrel Pool without getting a single rise or any sign of fish, some poachers arrived with a net and took 32 salmon out of it.

On another occasion the same gentleman had better luck. When walking home near Caen - after a blank day - he met the 'Kainer' (river bailiff) who commiserated with him on his bad luck, then lay down on the bank, put his hand into the water and threw out a grilse on the bank, with the remark that it would be something for him to take home!

One of the bankers went out for a day's fishing but, at the very commencement of the day, slipped and got soaking wet. He just divested himself of his clothing, and put it on bushes while he went ahead with the day's sport - obviously not plagued by midges or tourists.

Various superstitions seemed to be associated with the sport. Rods when assembled, must never be stepped over; this foreboded bad luck.

In a letter there is a reference to shooting hares for 3 days which resulted in a "bag" that filled a cart.

To get a greater range, e.g. for duck, shot in home-filled cartridges were enclosed in a wire cage before being loaded into the cartridge case. This is understood to have increased the effective range by over 20 yards.

Safety measures were rigidly enforced. Cartridges had to be withdrawn before crossing a fence, dyke or ditch, or when standing talking to anyone, and a gun must never be pointed in anyone's direction. "It is always a so-called empty gun that kills someone," was the constant cry.

No details of the overall level of bags shot in the Helmsdale area are available, but the details kindly provided by the Borrobol Estate detailed in Table L show these to have varied very considerably. In 1880 no fewer than 2106 brace of grouse and 4 stags were shot, whilst in 1994 no grouse at all were shot, but 91 stags were taken.

There are many reasons for this which are beyond the scope of this book. One possibility may be changes in land use e.g. afforestation; the drop in numbers of grazing sheep and particularly of hill cattle, where today the estate has only about thirty; not to mention the rise in real payroll costs of managing grouse moors.

VIII SCHOOLS AND EDUCATION

Until the Burgh Police (Scotland) Act of 1833 the education of the young was still very much a matter for the Established Church and was governed by the definitive Act of 1696. In each parish the heritor (the local landowner) was required by law to provide at least one school, the meagre salary of the schoolmaster and a house where he could live. By 1832 there was at least one such school in every parish, supplemented in many cases by a school provided by the Society in Scotland for the Propagation of Christian Knowledge - otherwise the SSPCK.

Beginning in 1825, General Assembly schools were also set up and by 1865 there were 200 such schools for which the General Assembly provided £5 to £25 per annum as a salary whilst the heritors provided a building for the school and a croft for the teacher (or its equivalent in money).

With these less-than-formal arrangements, it was inevitable that, from time to time, such relatively large covered areas should be used for purposes which might not be looked on as strictly educational. One such purpose for which such schools were used, was the annual cockfight, Whilst there is no trace of such an event happening in the Helmsdale school, it was very definitely held in Dornoch. For the report of this we are indebted to Donald Sage who was at school there in 1801. His experience, incidentally, was very similar to (if slightly more formal than) a happening in which Mr James Campbell, the future Helmsdale "dominie", was involved when he was teaching in Benbecula, in 1848.

Usually held in the parochial school, on Shrove Tuesday (or "Fastern's E'en") - but, for some reason, in Dornoch these were held instead in the Sheriff Court - proceedings commenced with the children arriving with cocks begged or borrowed for the "fight", to determine whose was to be "king" i.e. whose bird got the most victories, and the "queen", i.e. whose bird was runner up. Any bird who would not fight when placed on the stage was described as a "fugie", and became the property of the schoolmaster.

"Coronation Day" followed, usually on Candlemas Old Style, (about 13th February). This was held in the school premises, and after their crowning, the king and queen chose their lifeguards. A suitable exhortation from the dominie (in Latin!) followed, and then the procession went through the town behind the drum and fyfe. The proceedings terminated with a ball and supper in the evening.

If we ignore the SSPCK school at Caen in the late 18th century, its classes apparently held at one time in the former Kildonan church, and the possible "chant" school at Kiliain Church in pre-Reformation times, it seems likely the first one room school was in a store just over the river from the Church of Kiliain in 1835. The next would be beside the schoolhouse in Dunrobin Street, and would be followed by the new building known to have been put up near the new St. John's Kirk around 1840. A girls school, known to exist somewhere about the same date, may have moved into the recently vacated premises in Dunrobin Street.

With the opening of the new Church of St. John in 1841, it seems more than probable that this new building would form what was to become the base unit of the school that was to last till 1955. This would mean it would be available, shortly before Mr James Campbell came to the village, first in 1851 as a General Assembly teacher, and then as the teacher in the Parish School.

The population was continually growing, so it is no surprise to find that in 1871 another room was added. Two classrooms and a bell tower were added in 1883, two more rooms in 1892, a playground shelter in 1898, a science room in 1904, two classrooms in 1921, a gymnasium in 1930, a dining hall and kitchen in 1949, and a woodwork room in 1950.

It seems incredible that with the curriculum extended to include Latin in 1871, in the same year as the scheme for piped water in the village was completed, and with a house on the opposite side of the road connected with running water in 1881, practical hygiene was unknown in the school. So bad was it that, in 1894, something like fifty years after the school opened, a report by an inspector publicised for the first time that "there is no water within a hundred yards of school, and children are filthy in extreme"- surely a very sad reflection on the management capabilities of the School Board. As an attempt to remedy this, drinking water was provided in buckets and basins, which in turn resulted in the following logbook entry "Ten pails of water are now available...two boys amused themselves spitting and otherwise despoiling this. The punishment will probably prevent a repetition". At this time most children went barefoot in the summer.

In 1886, fees were reduced to 1/- per quarter, and "the tawse had been confirmed as official instrument of correction".

There was great excitement in 1904 when the science apparatus arrived, just in time for pupils (and staff!) to see the partial eclipse of the sun in the next year.

The old buildings became a Higher Grade School in 1908, and then a Senior Secondary School in 1938. When the new school was completed in 1955 it housed 134 primary, and 61 secondary pupils. In 1962 third year "academics" were removed to Golspie, to be followed in 1973 by all remaining third year pupils.

Up to this time the ten headmasters who had worked there were as follows:-

James Campbell	1854 - 1881
J. Matheson	1881 - 1891
John Munro	1891 - 1897
H. G. Robertson	1897 - 1910
W. Munro	1910 - 1935
A. W. MacKay	1935 - 1945
John Cook	1945 - 1953
Jas. S. Cunningham	1953 - 1959
David J. Bates	1960 - 1968
Alex. I. Blance	1968 - 1986

In the early part of the 19th century, Government grants paid to schools were made up of three main elements. The first of these was the number on the school roll, the second was the achievement of satisfactory results in the eyes of the inspectors, and thirdly the level of average attendances. The scales varied over the years but the following is one example of the basis adopted:-

Primary School

Average attendance	6/6d
Infants	8/-
Passes in reading, writing and arithmetic per subject.	3/-

Advanced Division

Passes in Maths, English, Latin and French (per subject)	4/-
Domestic Science	2/-

Pupil Teacher grant (each)	£2 - £3

Use of pupil teachers followed from the 1846 legislation which authorised pupils over 13 to assist primary teachers until they reached the age of 17. Not that they were only there to teach, they also had to be taught. This was accomplished by such means as the following example of a timetable adopted by the Dominie:-

a) Weekdays

8 a.m. to 9 a.m.	instruct the P.T.s and senior pupils;
9 a.m. to 4 p.m.	in the main school;
4 p.m. to 5 p.m.	seniors and pupil teachers;

b) Saturdays Seniors and P.T.s from 9.a.m till midday.

Use of pupil teachers ceased in Helmsdale in 1871.

With attendance levels an overriding factor, absences due to epidemics, attending/helping with the herring fishing, gathering whelks, or being at week-long Sacraments must have created difficulties for the head teacher. Some instances of these are given in Table M.

Day to day aspects of running the school were bound by the fact that the heritors and the Church of Scotland were responsible for meeting the cost of providing the parish school and furnishings, the salary of the teacher and such other incidentals as the cleaning of the school.

They kept all their expenditure to the minimum and in the 1850s the teacher's salary was £35 per year. Of course, in addition to this, the teacher was entitled to his teaching fees (when he could collect them). These started at 1d per week and then advanced by a half penny to 3d for the senior classes. Besides paying the fees, the pupils were supposed to purchase their textbooks and slates, which were ordered and paid for by the school master in the first instance. Somewhat unusually, as in most cases the Kirk Session was also involved, in Helmsdale the heritor seems to have been solely responsible for paying the school fees for orphans and for widows' children.

Pupils were supposed to bring a peat, a lump of coal or a log to supply the heating for the school. Those who forgot or omitted to bring their share, were placed at the back of the room, and probably also had a little external heating applied. The best quills of local geese were handed to the Dominie to provide the pens. To help him do this he kept his penknife constantly whetted, so it became automatic that when he entered a joiner's shop, an oil stone would be pushed over to him.

Most of the schoolwork was done on slates. The headings on the copy books had to be written in by the Dominie, and woe betide anyone who disfigured them. In addition to the usual primary subjects, Latin, French, Greek, Euclid (geometry), Algebra and Advanced Mathematics were taught - all on a salary of under £50 p.a.! With large numbers under the control of one teacher, discipline was strict, but did not depend solely on the belt. Punishment for smoking in school meant that the pupil had to smoke, to the bitter end, a clay pipe filled with 'Bogie Roll'. Sickness brought no remission; the pipe was re-lit and finally, the offender had to clean up the floor.

The first dominie, Mr James Campbell, used snuff (so much so that he earned himself the nickname of "Snuffy"). On one occasion he sent a boy to have his snuffbox refilled. The boy added some cayenne pepper. Nothing was said at the time but that evening Mr Campbell went out of his way to meet the boy's father and offered him a pinch. When he had recovered from its effects, the father was informed that this was his son's idea of a joke. The prank was not repeated.

Extracts from the school log books shown in Table N will give some idea of day to day events. Behind all those bland factual statements there must lie an absolute mass of stories of human interest. One story concerns the Sutherland Estates who did not want to be out of pocket for school fees, so they invoiced these to the crofters, along with rental and other dues.

Inspectors were the bane of a local teacher's existence. For grant purposes these gentlemen had to visit the schools annually, usually having to spend at least one night in the village. One such inspector complained about the "privies" (remember there were no water closets) so the schoolmaster was quick to point out that the inspector was unaware of the playground being a public thoroughfare. There were no locks on the doors of the privies and so they "stand invitingly open to the public." Another inspector had rather a thirst and, on one occasion, having wined and dined well, if not wisely, the evening before his inspection, submitted an unfavourable report. On his next visit, he returned to the same hostelry for some stimulant after his journey, to find the proprietor would not serve him unless he was accompanied by the schoolmaster. He raved and stormed at this and threatened to get in touch with the police, only to be told that the police sergeant had already stationed himself just outside in the hall.

This time there were no problems with the report.

On another occasion an inspector stressed that a head teacher should be fully conversant with all the subjects taught in his school. A needlework class was in progress, so the head teacher picked up a sock and turned the heel. He took another and handed it to the inspector, who had not the faintest idea how to set about it. The head, with his tongue well in his cheek, had great pleasure in asking how an inspector could dare to inspect something he could not do himself!

When the School Boards took over, there was immediate friction as the members thought that they knew how the school should be run. On one occasion, they invaded the school and made the head lose his temper. He had a bundle of copy books under his arm and, as he looked round for a safe repository, the board members fled the rising storm. The chairman was the last to reach the door, and banged it shut to hinder the pursuit. Unfortunately, he always wore a tail-coat. One of the tails got caught in the door jamb and he left it behind him.

The same pompous individual, when in the local bank, asked the cashier what he would do if anyone attempted to rob the bank. What he had not realised was that the cashier was not only an enthusiastic member of the volunteers, but also an expert pistol shot, so he was somewhat taken aback, when the banker pulled a loaded pistol from under the counter, and put a bullet through the inquisitor's silk hat.

We come now to the schools which were run by the Free Church. Many parents of that denomination refused to send their families to the Parish School after the Disruption, preferring (much to the astonishment of the Duke of Sutherland) that their children should have no education at all. Once they had their own system up and running however, it worked very well indeed. Unfortunately, from an historian's point of view, the form in which their statistics survive is not always explicit, as frequently what they describe as "Helmsdale" also includes various schools in the surrounding area.

What we do know is that in 1854 there were two Free Church schools in Helmsdale, one a general school sited where the Free Church now stands, (roll 110), and a Female School (roll 26) in Dunrobin Street.

The ultimate smooth running of the Free Church schools was achieved by appointing a Free Church Presbyterial Education Committee in 1843. This body was able to have a Free Church school opened at Loth in the next year, and one at Portgower in the year following, but it was only in 1846 that the principal Free Church school opened in Helmsdale. The other, a School of Industry for Girls, had opened in the previous year just opposite the present Community Centre, and it says much for the devotion of the teacher, Mrs. Campbell, that she worked there, without pay, for two years. By 1847 the Helmsdale-based Free Church Schools (these include Portgower and Loth) had 324 pupils, and it was agreed only then, that Mrs Campbell should receive a salary.

Gradually it was appreciated that running two parallel education systems in such a small country as Scotland had many disadvantages, and in 1850 an overture was made by Free Church Presbytery of Dornoch to the General Assembly of the Free Church for speedy establishment of a system of National Education. A petition was made to Parliament on the same lines in 1853, but it was to be almost twenty years before a national scheme came into being.

By 1863 the overall Free Church school rolls amounted to 249. In 1864 additional information states that "[in Helmsdale] there is a Free Church school (roll 110), and a Free Church Female School (roll 26), whilst at Loth there is a Parish School (roll 42). At Portgower there were both a General Assembly School (roll 37 all from Free Church families) and a Free Church school with a roll of 50".

Because of prevailing fever, the 1870 inspection of the Free Church School at Helmsdale did not take place. In 1881 both the Helmsdale Free Church schools closed, and pupils transferred to Helmsdale East school, although the former Free Church school at Portgower continued for about another two years

For some reason the leasehold tenures granted by the Sutherland Estates to the Free Churches at Helmsdale and at Rogart for both their schools and their Church buildings, were only for a period of 57 years instead of usual 99 years.

In the 19th century the services of teachers were called on for many extramural purposes, calculating such things as the quantities in hay stacks, or the amount of "road metal" broken by itinerant workers. Also they helped with correspondence for the many adults who could not read or write fluently.

Whilst not situated in Helmsdale itself, another educational establishment was a great asset to the village. This was Golspie Technical School opened in 1904 at the instigation of Duchess Millicent. Residential accommodation was available for 55 boys from all over the County and places were allocated on merit. In the mid 1970s this became an annexe of Golspie High School.

IX THE VOLUNTEERS

In 1859 Napoleon III was starting to make very warlike noises, and, whilst these were mainly against Austria, Great Britain began to get alarmed. In Scotland all traces of the Volunteers of 1803 and of the Sharpshooters of 1819 were but memories, so on 25th May 1859 the first steps were taken to set up new bands of Volunteers. Helmsdale was quick to respond and a unit of the 1st Sutherlandshire Royal Artillery Volunteers, was formed on 26th April 1860, with a corresponding unit formed at Golspie in 1867. Similarly units of the Rifle Corps were formed at Brora on 3rd Jan 1860, at Dornoch on 2nd December 1859, and at Rogart on 13th October 1860.

From 1863 to 1867 the Helmsdale-based unit was attached to 1st Inverness-shire Corps. It then became part of the 1st Caithness Administration Brigade.

Being an artillery unit, the Helmsdale corps was initially equipped with field guns as well as small arms, and later, with 32-pounder battery guns.

Fig. No. 13. Officers' Uniforms of
Sutherland and Caithness Volunteers.

With acknowledgements to late Maj. Gen. J M Grierson,
"Scottish Volunteer Force".

73

Fig. No. 14.
Guard of Honour from Volunteer Force. at Laying of Foundation Stone of Harbour 1892.
From collection of Mr. J. Jappy.

The uniform they adopted was similar to that of the Royal Artillery, but with scarlet cuffs, and white cord piping and belts. The busbies worn by the officers were unusual in that they had chin chains instead of the more usual leather strap (see Fig. No 13). These were replaced by field service or forage caps in 1894 (see Fig. 14).

Whilst some local men enjoyed a bit of shooting and a little rod fishing, this was not available to many, so the Volunteers became a means of popular activity.

The unit had a shooting range for rifle practice just down from the Caithness Road, and their cannon battery practised out to sea on towed targets. The exact location of the battery and the 300 yard rifle range can be seen in Fig. No. 15. The latter must have presented problems in 1873 when the unit was issued with Snider breech loading carbines "nicely sighted at 600 to 700 yards".

With the targets for the battery guns towed out to sea, it was enthralling to see the splashes in the water when the shells landed.

As we have seen, the unit was supervised from Wick. Much of the administration was conducted by letter and by telegram. Replies to letters were expected within 3 days - if not received, a telegram was dispatched to know the reason why.

Officers who did not own a saddle horse, and who required a charger for ceremonial purposes, had to borrow from a friend.

In those days a man's average earnings were about 12/- a week, so the fines imposed on a volunteer for breach of regulations must have been crippling. If he was caught pointing a rifle at another man, the fine was 2/- for the first offence, and 5/- for the second. In addition to the fine for the second offence, the offender was dismissed from the force. Great care was taken that all carbines were returned to the armoury after every shoot. Otherwise ammunition would be missing and the carbines used to poach deer.

Apart from the details of numbers attending local balls and other functions, there are no records available as to the numbers involved in Helmsdale itself; but in 1871, between Helmsdale and Golspie, the total established strength was 160 of which the numbers deemed efficient were 145.

Only the names of four commanding officers are known. These were William Houston (1873-75), David Sutherland (1875-78), Robert Hill (1878-82), and a Mr Shaw in 1908.

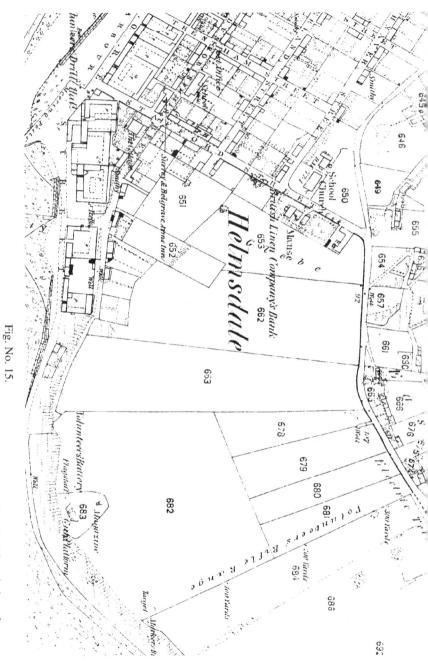

Fig. No. 15.
Map showing Situation of Volunteers Ranges, and original Volunteer Hall. Reproduced by Kind Permission of Trustees of National Library of Scotland.

76

The unit went to Dunrobin Castle annually for 'The Review' - always a very lively affair. They also went there when salutes were required for such high days as the visit of Queen Victoria or other notable or Royal personages.

Dunrobin apart, no formal event in the village was complete without the unit. The laying of the harbour foundation stone (See Fig. No. 14), the memorial service for Queen Victoria, and the first launching of the lifeboat all merited a parade.

For the annual review at Dunrobin, Volunteers were billeted in the Golspie drill hall. One year, part of this had been hired by the local hotel keeper as a store for his spare liquor for the bar. A wooden barricade had been erected but did not reach the ceiling. Consequently, next morning, some difficulty was experienced to get sufficient sober artillery men to fire the salutes!

Not everyone went to parades regularly, and many used their uniform trousers for off-duty purposes. These uniforms were made specially for each Volunteer by a firm in Inverness, 80% being paid by Sutherland Estates.

Sergeant instructors frequently lived in the village, but several of them suffered from the weakness of regulars of that period, and were often semi-alcoholics. Those so affected had to be dismissed. A bandmaster was supplied for the county and had to visit each unit in turn.

The local event of the year was the Volunteer Ball. This was held in the Drill Hall, and was usually attended by between thirty and forty Volunteers and partners. It was always still in full swing at 4 o'clock in the morning when the dominie would usually decide, if he was to face a crowded classroom the next day, he had better go home. Everyone else would go straight home around 6 a.m., change into working garb and go to work. Excesses of any kind were sternly repressed and reprimanded, though owners of stables near at hand generously permitted some who had succumbed, to sleep the effects off in their loft.

It is recorded that the Ball in 1871 was particularly good, helped, no doubt, by the gift of a gallon of whisky from Clyneleish distillery in Brora. Likewise the annual inspection of that year was also considered a success, and each man got a generous dram afterwards.

Unfortunately there was a blot in the copybook the next year when a sergeant went off with the funds of the unit "on a drunken binge".

The last Volunteer Ball was held in 1908 when the Commanding Officer was Lieutenant Shaw, and seems to have been attended by about 50 volunteers and partners.

What we now know as the Drill Hall in Dunrobin Street, although it is now used for commercial purposes, is not the one used by the original

Volunteers. It stood on the harbourside but was converted to use as a store in 1891, and incorporated in a curing yard. Its exact location can be seen in Fig. 14.

The unit was disbanded in 1908, when the Territorial Army concept was greeted with less than enthusiasm. Only 11 men came forward to join the new unit, compared with the turnout of approximately 60 for the laying of the harbour foundation stone some 15 years previously (see Fig. No. 13), but by the beginning of World War II it had become a very popular unit - partly because it provided almost the only means of getting a paid holiday. Needless to say, the men who went to camp were not "let off the hook" as wives and families followed them. The unit, the 5th Seaforth, are still entitled to wear the Sutherland tartan and the "cat" crest with the Sutherland motto "Sans Peur". This popularity, unfortunately, had another price to pay as can be seen from the list of names on the War Memorial.

One tradition passed down to the T.A. from the Volunteers, and maintained until 1939, was the Annual Ball. Usually held on New Year's night after a day on the range at Caen, everyone was very smartly turned out indeed, but perhaps the proceedings were a little more restrained than in "the Old Days"!

Fisher boys usually joined the R.N.V.R. For this they had an annual retainer, the amount of which varied over the years, but the fortnight's training at a suitable depot remained constant.

X GOLD

In 1868, Mr R N Gilchrist, a native of the Strath of Kildonan returned home from the Australian gold fields and realised the geology of his native Strath was very like that in which he had been digging for gold "down under". Maybe too there was some earlier knowledge of it. Donald Sage in his "Mermorabilia" recounts the story of gold in the Strath. He has the story that someone, being pursued in the Strath, had thrown a pot of gold he had panned into a water-filled hole near the road, and a single nugget had been found about 1820 in the Helmsdale river.

Be that as it may, with the permission of the 3rd Duke the prospector "tried his hand" and found quite material deposits of gold. The news spread. In the next year, 1869, the Duke was prevailed upon to grant prospecting licences. As a result there were soon about 500 men working in plots of about 40 square feet on the Kildonan and Kinbrace burns at a fee of £1 per month. In addition to this, there was also a royalty of £1 per ounce due to the Crown, with the best gold being found in the Suisgill burn.

Some of the men lived in huts (see photograph in Fig. No. 16) but many more lived in tents.

Much of the gold seems to have been encashed in Helmsdale where at least two dealers operated, and doubtless some of it was not declared to the Revenue inspectors. One of these dealers was Mr P G Wilson, who made it into jewellery, and the other who operated on an agency basis, was the Inspector of the Poor, Mr James Campbell. His purchases of gold went to Mr Naughten at Inverness, as did some of the purchases of garnets. It was from Mr Naughten that a ring of the Kildonan gold was ordered for the Prince of Wales.

It perhaps seems rather incongruous that in a letter to a local minister, Rev J MacPherson, advising against carrying coffins of fever victims, the local Sanitary Inspector also commented on a ring the minister possessed as "the best article [of Kildonan gold] I have ever seen".

Problems with unauthorised diggers and protests from both sportsmen and farmers over damage to the land and river banks resulted in the Duke putting an end to prospecting from 1st January 1870. Later that year three Helmsdale gentlemen met the Duke and tried to persuade him to change his mind, but this he was not prepared to do. In part, at least, this seems to have

Fig. No. 16.
Temporary Living Quarters at Bal an Or at time of Gold Rush (1868).
From Collection of the Wick Society.

been due to the Government refusing to send inspectors to monitor the position.

There was no further individual prospecting, but, in 1883 there is a comment that "A London Company has resumed [gold] mining at £10 per acre along the flat of the Suisgill burn, and is said to be doing rather well". Machines had been erected, but floods in 1886 ended the diggings, and the plant of the Sutherland Mining Co. was removed.

In the "rush" most of the miners "panned" for the gold; i.e. using a basin, placing some of the alluvial sediment in the basin and swilling it about in the water of the burn. The stones were thrown out and the sand gradually washed away leaving a deposit in the foot of the basin comprising magnetic iron ore, garnets and gold dust. The iron was removed with a magnet, and the garnets and the gold dust or nuggets collected. The dust was placed in containers containing a little water. Just how this was done can be seen in Timespan Heritage Centre, where a most illuminating scenario is displayed.

Fine gold dust is very lively, and would find its way out of a container if not both made inactive with the water and the container tightly corked. The coarse grains were put in quills (the precursors of the modern phial) and tightly stoppered.

The garnets also had a ready market for jewellery.

A great many 'poachers' omitted to obtain licences and interdicts were obtained against some of these as can be gathered from the Sheriff Court records which show that in April 1869 the Duke took out 33 decrees of interdict against just such persons.

When panning came to an end each of the miners reacted in individual ways. One digger by the name of Fraser sent his wife and children home, bought two ankers of whisky, and went on a binge for a week ("the darkie included"). Another, George Leask, went off to Aberdeen clutching his total take of 40 ounces (over three pounds or a kilo and a half in weight), for which he expected to get about 63/- to 65/- an ounce - surprisingly somewhat less than the 68/- that had been offered to David Sutherland, of Wilson Street, Wick about the same time. The usual price seemed to be about £3.3/- to £3.12/- an ounce.

Today, panning is still a weekend and tourist attraction, and has been known to be not unprofitable!

XI RAILWAY

In the 1860s the 3rd Duke of Sutherland could see the advantage to the fishing industry of a rail link from Helmsdale to the south, but by 1868 the Sutherland & Caithness Railway Company had only managed to get their line as far north as Golspie, some six miles short of the intended terminus of Brora. Accordingly the Duke decided to build his own line from Golspie to Helmsdale, and put in motion the various legal steps required to obtain the necessary private Act of Parliament.

The Act was not passed until 20th June 1870, but once it was apparent there would be little opposition to his proposals, the 3rd Duke got on with the tracklaying, so providing some very welcome employment for those hit by the slump in the herring catch. Very soon temporary stations were constructed at Dunrobin and at Helmsdale, so he was able to have the private line formally opened by Princess Christian in November 1870.

As this line was not connected to the main track south, the Duke's engine is thought to have been landed at Helmsdale by sea, and towed up to the station by traction engines. The carriages were brought by train to Golspie and then pulled along the road to Dunrobin also by traction engines.

Initially, it seemed the requisite Helmsdale firing of the Royal Salute at the opening of the railway by Princess Beatrice, might cause problems as there was no ammunition for battery guns, field guns being considered inappropriate. A telegram to Dunrobin produced the necessary ammunition for a battery salute by the Volunteers, just in the nick of time.

From that opening, until the joining with the main line some six months later, a service of two trains each way ran daily (Sundays excepted) between Helmsdale and Dunrobin, and the staff at Dunrobin Castle acquired at least one other member in the form of an engine driver. The Duke enjoyed being fireman when available! All trains called at Brora, and the journey of just over 16 miles took 45 minutes.

Nor was he the only member of the household to be involved. One of the Duke's family, when typing a letter about some of these moves, described her task as a "Lenten Penance"!

The finally completed track to the south was opened on June 19th 1871. It cost £3,700 per mile to complete and at the time was said to be "the cheapest of construction in the United Kingdom" in spite of the fact that was stressed in the report, that the men had ben "paid wages by the Duke and not on the odious truck system". The construction work involved had included 37 bridges, 3 miles of new roads, 318,000 cubic yards of excavation and 65,000 cubic yards of ballasting.

Until 1895 the Duke ran his private train using a small 2-4-0 tank engine called "Dunrobin" built by Kitson & Co., Leeds which ended its life as the "Gordon Castle", working from Fochabers and Invergordon.

The replacement (also named Dunrobin) was a more powerful 0-4-4 tank engine, built by Atlas Works, Glasgow in 1895 (see Fig. No. 17). Like its predecessor it was named "Dunrobin" and was painted dark green. One of the features installed by the 4th Duke who ordered it, was a seat with leather cushions which extended the full width of the engine. This was used by distinguished visitors, of whom there were many. Their names were recorded on the front weather board, and range from Princess Beatrice in 1870 to Neville Chamberlain in 1938. This board can still be seen in Dunrobin Castle.

Another unusual feature providing for the creature comforts of these visitors, were two lunch boxes with hinged lids, situated under the footplate.

The luxury carriage from the Duke's private train, and the small carriage he used locally, were usually kept at Dunrobin Station but the engine "Dunrobin 2" was usually kept at Helmsdale where it could be more easily maintained. All three items are still in existence - the luxury carriage in the York Railway Museum and the latter two artefacts in British Columbia at Fort Steele Museum.

Besides the engine, the initial rolling stock included the small carriage of brake wagon type (if somewhat more luxurious in its fitting out), but the 4th Duke also wanted better rolling stock for his trips south when it was attached to the timetabled main services, so he commissioned Wolverton Carriage Works to produce a suitable vehicle. This was 61 feet long, and included a lounge, a smoking room, three bedrooms, a pantry and an attendants compartment (See Fig. No. 18). When being used as part of his own small train, the original small carriage was also attached and was used as a steadying vehicle at the rear. Only in 1948 was the privilege of the Duke so using the main line trains withdrawn.

When he was Prince of Wales, King Edward VII travelled in this coach, and used it and the engine "Dunrobin 2", as the prototype of the Royal Train built in 1903.

Extracts from a press report of the May 1871 opening of the track may

Fig. No. 17.
Duke of Sutherland's Dunrobin Engine No 2.
By Courtesy of Railway Magazine.

Fig. No. 18.
Duke of Sutherland's Saloon Carriage.
By Courtesy of Railway Magazine.

be of interest. "There [were] great doings here for the opening of the railway to Helmsdale...... A luncheon, tickets 10/-, was given to the Duke of Sutherland..... The children who had been placed inside the fence opposite the station to greet the arrival of the train, were given a treat in the evening."

The 3rd Duke really enjoyed being involved in his engine shed, and there is a delightful story told of a "local" who was standing talking to a friend, and ignoring another oily individual working nearby. Only when he rudely criticised the Sutherland family, and received a punch on the jaw, did he realise this was the Duke himself!

When the track was linked to Inverness and Thurso, the small engineering shop which the Duke had set up at Brora as an ancillary to the operation, was moved to a smaller shed, and in 1884 the original engine shed turned into a wool carding and spinning operation was leased to a Yorkshire firm. This project was later taken over in 1901 by Mr T M Hunter from Galashiels, who until then had been running a wool mill in Wick. He rapidly built the business up and was soon taking wool from as far away as Skye, but unlike MacNaughtons of Pitlochry with whom he was in competition, he did not seem to use his travelling representatives to measure for, and to take orders for personal tweed garments. The same Mr Hunter went on to launch the Brora Electric Supply Co Ltd. in 1913. This kept the village supplied with current until 1938.

During both World Wars Helmsdale station provided not only water for the engines passing through, but also refreshments for servicemen on board. This was particularly true of the trains which were nicknamed the Jellicoes, (Jellies, or Jellicans for short). Named after the first World War Admiral of that name, originally one ran daily (except Sundays) in each direction between Thurso and Euston, but in the 1940s there was also a certain element of duplication.

Each train had two locomotives and an incredible number of carriages, all filled to absolute capacity, including the corridors. They stopped at Helmsdale about 7 a.m. going north and about 7 p.m. going south. There, WVS personnel were waiting with their great urns of tea, as well as such more solid refreshments as could be gathered together in those days of rationing. Many ladies were involved in this operation over the years, but the only names now known are Mrs Traill of the grocers family, Mrs MacLaren, wife of the stationmaster, and Mrs Finlayson, wife of one of the drivers.

In the 1914-18 war two locomotives the "Snaigow" and the "Durn" were specially built for the run, whilst in the last war, "Black Fives" were the usual lead loco.

With such a punishing schedule there were bound to be some "incidents". Because of the tight security that surrounded the operation, only a few details of these have leaked out. On one very cold night, a short signal stop at Balavil ended in a stop of several hours when the wheels froze to the track and an "eight coupler" had to push start it. Weather also affected the journey on one night in January 1942 when a train took four days to get from Inverness to Thurso, because it became snow-bound between Forsinard and Kinbrace. After the heating failed, food and blankets were dropped from aircraft.

On another occasion seven carriages came off the track at Thurso because of line-spread, and one night at Inverness two much overloaded trucks with flattened springs had to be taken off at Inverness. (It is thought their contents consisted of gold from Russia).

Naturally local boys on board were given special treatment, and it was wonderful what could be achieved if they had the foresight to send a telegram saying "Jelly Thursday" or some similar cryptic message.

In addition to the regular stations at Golspie and Brora, several of the sporting estates arranged their own halts in the strath to the north of Helmsdale, and of course the Duke had his own private station at Dunrobin where there were two waiting rooms, one for the family and Royalty, and one for "others". The original wooden shelter was replaced in 1874 by a half-timbered building. This was restored in 1990 by the joint efforts of British Rail and the Sutherland family, and, in 1997 was completely renovated by the Estate and Mr Britain-Caitlin from Scotscalder in Caithness. Part of the waiting area now has a display of railway artefacts.

Today, when Helmsdale station is a completely unmanned request stop, it seems incredible to recall that up to 1961, seventy-seven men were employed there to service the engines and to deal with the traffic; but at least, despite threats to close the line, the traveller in 1998 can still come to Helmsdale from Inverness by rail!

XII ANOTHER HELMSDALE MURDER

On the night of 4th August 1817 Margaret Mackay from Loth had been sleeping in Helmsdale Toll House. She was disturbed by what she described as "roaring of cows in the field", and, looking out the window she saw a woman lying on the ground in such a position as to indicate that all was not well. She roused the others in the house, who went to the assistance of the woman, brought her in, and put her to bed where a gash in her head was dressed by Donald Mackenzie, a travelling salesman, another temporary overnight resident.

By this time the victim was recognised as Catherine Sutherland "alias Ogg", who remained in the tollhouse until 9 p.m. that evening, when she was carried to the house of John Farrel (presumably a relation), a fisherman in Easter Helmsdale. There she died next morning.

Statements were taken the next day by the Sheriff Substitute, from local people who seemed to have something relevant to say, and also from William Ross from Cambusmore the surgeon who had examined the body. This examination had revealed a cut in the forehead of the body through which he "could put two fingers into the substance of the brain and...... that this was the cause of her death". The cut, he thought had been inflicted with a blunt, but thin edged instrument.

He also said he had found lacerations on the right arm deep enough to expose the muscles and tendons of the arm, probably caused by the same instrument.

Ann Murray, wife of John Mackay, a fisherman, was able to tell that early on the morning in question she had been going past the tollhouse and saw Adam Mackay nearby with a spade in his hand repeating the words "I'll murder her, I'll murder her, I'll murder her".

Another William Ross, this time a cooper, told the Sheriff that about six o'clock that morning he had been walking near the harbour where he met Isobel MacDonald, with tears in her eyes who had told him about a woman lying in the toll house "who had been nearly murdered by Adam MacKay". He had immediately gone to the tollhouse to render such assistance as he could, and had not been many minutes there when he observed Adam MacKay walking past the gable of the house making towards the garden, from where he returned carrying a spade. MacKay had come to the tollhouse door, but because "he was thought to be out of his senses, the door had been

Fig. No. 19
Toll House at Helmsdale Bridge where Catherine Sutherland alias Ogg was found dying in 1817.
Reproduced by permission of the Records of Scotland: Ref. JC26/383.

kept locked against him". He then went with the toll keeper "and tied up his hands" for safety.

About an hour after all this happened Adam Mackay was found (still with his hands tied) "trying to walk along the roofs of houses and other dangerous places" so William Ross took him to his sister's house in Wester Helmsdale where he was left in her care with his hands still bound.

The grandson of the tollkeeper confirmed that the evening before the murder, when Adam Mackay was in to his father's house (not the tollhouse) in a very troublesome mood, chasing various people and threatening to strike them, he had tied Mackay's hands together with the help of George Sutherland and John Polson. Then they had taken him to his (Adam MacKay's) mother's house at Elderable, but had later learned MacKay had escaped from there early next morning.

Adam Mackay was formally charged with the murder but at the criminal trial held in Inverness on 24th September 1817. After "having been enclosed in an adjoining room for a few minutes" the jury found the charge "Not Proven".

In passing it is interesting that in another source, the keeper (described at the trial as a toll gatherer) at Helmsdale Toll is reported to have had such a good income providing overnight accommodation and refreshment (mainly in the form of illicit whisky), that he was lax in his duty of collecting tolls for crossing the bridge.

The then tollhouse was a small "butt and ben" situated at the north end of the bridge, on the east side of the road. (see Fig. No. 19).

XIII FINANCING THE ESTATE DEVELOPMENTS

We have seen how in the nineteenth century Sutherland Estates put a lot of time and trouble into the construction of new villages and roads. Partly because of the accounting system adopted, and partly because some of the factors took their papers with them when they left, just how much was spent in this way will never be known exactly. What we can do, however, is to use the facts we have to form an estimate of what was involved.

We know, for example that the average costs of the Telford roads was £450 per mile; that the laying of the railtrack cost about £3,700 per mile; improving the castle cost about £64,000; and that the amount spent establishing the village of Brora was in the region of £30,000.

On this basis, to establish 500 miles of road, 17 miles of rail track and the infrastrucrure of the villages of Helmsdale, Golspie and Brora must have cost in the region of £500,000. Not that this would be all spent at the same time. It would be spread out over about 20 years.

From 1803 until his death in 1833 the first Duke (or the Marquess of Stafford as he was for most of the period) had a really colossal income. From his canal profits alone he seems to have had an average of £64,000 per annum, and to this would fall to be added the net rental income from his various estates as well as the dividends from his railway shares. One estimate has put the total of these at one time at £200,000 but just how accurate that may be is not known.

A lot of this money was spent on maintaining his various houses and in giving receptions in London. Perhaps the most telling comment on the standard to which all of this was done was made by Queen Victoria who remarked when attending one reception that she felt she was coming from her house to the Sutherland palace.

Coincidentally, it was in 1803, the same year as the Marquess received his inheritance and decided to improve the estate, that the Parliamentary Commissioners for Roads and Bridges appointed Thomas Telford to head up the task of providing the Highlands with a proper system of roads and bridges, so this meant his services were available on the spot, so to speak, to the Sutherland Estates.

All Telford's roads were built with cattle droving in mind, so they were 15' wide and well bottomed under a gravel top surface of from 12 - 16 inches, and so also suitable for carriages.

In todays terms the above cost figures are practically meaningless, but it will perhaps convey more to the reader if they are adjusted for the inflation that has taken place since. This can only be done using a very "broad brush" but it is probably true to say that, in addition to the sums spent relieving hunger in times of need, the Estates outlays represented about £250 million overall, and the canal profits which accrued to the Marquess were about £30 million annually.

Fig. No. 20.
Plaque on Wall of House
erected by Sutherland Estates.

XIV LIFE IN THE COMMUNITY

We have seen how the various elements of fishing, crofting and "huntin' and fishin'", combined to produce quite a reasonable, if erratic, source of revenue for the village which had sprung up as a result of William Young's report of 1810. What we have not yet looked at is how life in general went on.

Although according to the plan in Fig. No. I, building was not supposed to start until 1814, some construction must have started about 1812 because in that year tiles were shipped from Peterhead to Helmsdale at a cost of £23 14s 10d, and in the next year £47 19s 3d. In that year, too, a toll house was erected, which as we have seen in Chapter XII was the site of a brutal murder in 1817.

We know nothing else specific until 1816 when the Commercial Hotel was erected (later to become Ross's Hotel, and today the Bridge Hotel - not to be confused with the Ross's Hotel which functioned next door in the 1930s), with Mr George Alexander of Golspie completing the Surrey and Belgrave Arms in 1819 (now the Belgrave Arms).

From the point of view of local business use, the latter was in the best position, with the Kiliain Parish Church manse to the west, the schoolhouse, which was to become the Registrar's office almost opposite, and the offices of the Customs and Fishery officers just down the hill. The sites of some of these can be identified today by the coats of arms of the Sutherlands which appear on the exterior of the houses in question. A photograph of one of those remaining is shown in Fig. No. 20.

This particular crest is in two parts, and is thought to represent the Coat of Arms of George Leveson Gower, Viscount Trentham and his wife. In 1785 he had married Elizabeth, Countess of Sutherland in her own right, but the coronet on the left as you look at it is that of an English Marquis, whilst that on the right seems to be appropriate to a Marchioness as the wife of a Marquis.

Naturally these locations did not continue indefinitely. The Session Clerk (later the Registrar) moved his premises, first further to the east in Dunrobin Street, and then to Bunillidh Cottage in Old Caithness Road, whilst the Kiliain Manse was superseded by the St. John's manse in 1841. (point 2 on the map in Fig. No. 10).

Completion of the Surrey and Belgrave Arms coincided with the initiation of the stagecoach service from Inverness to Wick, and marks the beginning of the running down of the direct managerial supervision of day-to-day happenings by the Sutherland Estates. At the same period a butcher from Kirriemuir started to operate in the village on a part-time seasonal basis. At the height of the herring season he was killing two to three bullocks a week. He was also a trained weaver.

The next major development about which we know anything is the 1825 establishment of a distillery by A. & D. Simpson, whose family had originally come from the Moray coast. They had traded as fishcurers and also had farming interests on what is now the A9 road, just to the north of the village at Boghals. By 1831 the distillery was taken over by a slightly different consortium, Alexander Simpson & Co. which completely renewed the plant (see plan in Fig. No. 2).

In 1837 Alexander Simpson died and the new grouping of James Christie & Co. took over. This they seem to have done without proper investigation because the distillery was probably insolvent even then.

By 1840 both the struggling distillery and its associated brewery had closed, and Jas. Christie & Co. was sequestrated. This was not their only business interest as they had a wholesale grocers and wine merchants business in Golspie, where they were local agents for Aberdeen Town and Country Bank. From the Bank they seem to have embezzled some very large sums of money. The partners tried to abscond, but were arrested in London, just as they were about to flee to Gibraltar on SS "Iberia".

After this episode an attempt was made to run the distillery as an offshoot of the Pultneytown Distillery in Wick, but this did not last long.

A few years earlier, a lime kiln was established to west of the distillery. At almost the same time, in 1832, a temporary hospital was constructed nearby to cope with victims of a severe cholera outbreak in which the local doctor and about 40 others perished. As a result there are a number of little-known unmarked burials in the cemetery. So strong was local feeling, that crews of boats from the south who had been unfortunate enough to have some of their number die on passage, were not allowed to bring bodies ashore for burial. In the same epidemic in Wick, there were 306 cases of cholera and 66 fatalities. This same cholera epidemic seems to have resulted in little known unmarked burials in the cemetery, and in the strath at Loth where it wiped out almost all the inhabitants.

Two years later, 1834 saw a mail gig start to run regularly from Inverness to Wick. On its first journey to the north, with the driver and passengers being welcomed with drams at every stop, its course was somewhat erratic - definitely the first case of drunk driving in Sutherland! Not that such a scale of drinking was unusual, because in 1851, as a result of the large amount of drunkenness at weekends, the Duke of Sutherland reduced the number of drinking houses in Helmsdale from six to five.

Up to this time the relief of the poor had been the responsibility of the Church and then in 1845 the Parish Council took over. This more or less heralded the modern system of Local Government, with the responsibility passing to local ratepayers in the form of Parochial Boards. The first meeting of Helmsdale Parochial Board was held in the house of Thomas Jackson, Caen. At this various members of the Board were appointed, including Adam Couper of whom we will hear more later.

When the 19th century records are examined, we get some idea not only of what real poverty was, but also how local families were accustomed to care for their poorer relatives, the old and the sick. The minute of a meeting of the Board in Ross's Inn (now the Bridge Hotel) in 1859 lists 80 paupers (15 male and 65 female) with 14 male and 16 female dependents. One of the cases dealt with was a lunatic out on licence, living in a crowded room with only two beds in which slept his mother, father and two sisters. A room had been made available elsewhere with the necessary bedding but the family refused to let him go.

A few years later, to cut costs by saving rents, paupers were to be housed two to a room instead of one "until the Barracks [the poor-house] is filled".

Similarly, in 1860 some clothing and other effects handed out to paupers who had subsequently died, were transferred from the deceased to living paupers. Items listed for such treatment were blankets, bedcovers, flannel shifts, stockings, feather pillows, towels, petticoats, and shoes.

When a pauper died the finances available did not allow for the provision of a coffin, so the body was wrapped in a shroud and transported to the grave in a special basket. Examples of these baskets can be seen in the museum in Dunrobin Castle.

An attempt was made to clear up the condition of the streets, and a contractor was prepared to pay £20 per annum for the right to lift manure he found there.

Even more legislation was brought into force in 1856 when Session

Clerks automatically became Registrars of Births, Deaths, and Marriages. In Helmsdale the person involved was Mr James Campbell, who was to hold the post for almost sixty years.

Smallpox was always a worry, and in 1861 Dr Rutherford, the official vaccinator for the Parish, reported to a somewhat concerned Board that vaccinations for the year numbered 714 but only 305 were successful. At the same meeting the treasurer pointed out that the amount paid to registered poor for the year was £373 4/- an increase of £52 16/- "because of large families left by deceased paupers".

A great step forward was taken in 1865 when it was agreed that £5587 be borrowed by Parochial Board to found Combination Poorhouses. At this time the "Barracks" building was already available in Helmsdale.

Two years later, in 1867, James Campbell was appointed Collector of Rates and Inspector of the Poor. One of the first things he had to deal with was an individual application to the Parochial Board for a pair of drawers and a pair of shoes! At the same meeting as this request was dealt with, it was agreed that a wheelbarrow, shovel and scraper should be bought for the scavenger, and that street manure should be uplifted twice weekly by horse and cart except in herring season, when it was to be done daily.

Things were going from bad to worse when in 1868 it was found that the Barracks Poorhouse was in such bad condition that, if it was not improved, paupers could not continue occupation. In the next year H. M. Inspectors of Schools condemned the schoolhouse as substandard, so it seemed some tightening up was required by the Parochial Board. Included in the measures introduced was one that required all common lodging houses to be regulated.

Taken together, these may have been the factors which influenced Major General George Pope, Navidale Cottage, who when he died in 1885 bequeathed funds for the establishment of a small medical dispensary in the village. Obviously the wheels of the concerned Local Government departments. must have ground very slowly as it opened in 1935, some 50 years later! At that time it was a general hospital, but under the National Health Service it became a maternity unit, which in 1951 saw 88 babies brought into the world. On economic grounds it was closed altogether in 1977, and is now a private residence.

Towards the end of the century we have indications of two banks opening. Of one we know little, but it seems to have been a branch office of the North of Scotland Town and Country Bank, known locally as the Thurso Town and Country Bank.

The other was the British Linen Bank which opened first as a branch office from Golspie (1868) at the time of the gold rush, but achieved independent status in 1875 under the management of J. J. Hill who remained in office until 1918; quite a record! He was followed by another local, Mr J O Levack, who retired in 1937. Located originally on the junction of Stafford Street and Strathnaver Street, the office later (in 1907) moved to the junction of Dunrobin Street and Stafford Street where the Bank of Scotland stands today .

About 1900 the parish population, both of Helmsdale and the landward area, was 1772. Ten years later it had risen to 1786 and by 1921 it was reduced to 1518. In 1981 it stood at 863.

The first six years of the 20th century saw plans submitted for the new Masonic Hall, for Coast Guard Houses and Watch Tower, for Police Station improvements, and for the construction of the carpet factory. 1906 was the year when a forty gallon illegal still was discovered in Strathcarron.

The aftermath and bravery of servicemen in the First World War was symbolised with the 1923 unveiling of the War Memorial, just beside the Telford Bridge. 1926 saw a brighter picture with the presentation of Castle Park to the village community by George Couper.

The parish population (then 1,454), must have felt they were taking a great step forward in 1933 when Mr J McLeod started a local electricity supply. He had no statutory obligation to supply everyone, so he fixed his own charges, and refused to give supplies to any premises not wired up by his own personnel. This situation resolved itself in 1950 when the supply was taken over and controlled by North of Scotland Hydro Electric Board.

At that time the population had fallen to 1,338. Two years later it was reported running water was now installed in all dwelling houses. In 1972 the new A9 road bridge over the Helmsdale River opened.

In the 1850s it is recorded that the village tradesman included 2 blacksmiths, 3 tailors, 3 bakers, 3 shoe makers, one butcher, and six grocers.

Today, a century and a half later some of individual prices may be of interest

Peat - per cart load	1/6d
Aquavite (whisky) - per bottle	1/6d
Aquavite (whisky) - per gallon	16/-
Trousers	18/6d
Coat.	8/6d
Coat - made to measure	£2. 2/-
Beef - 13 lbs.	4/10d
Pork - 16lbs	5/4d
Milk - per day	½d
Coal - per ton	16/-
Shirt - woollen	3/6d
Candles - 7ins	4/-
Shaving brush	10d
Curtain cloth - 17 yds	5/6d
Hair brush.	2/-
Fender & fire irons.	9/6d
Potatoes - per bag.	2/-
Meal - Firlot.	4/-

A suit length from Brora mills cost £1.1/-; making up cost £1.1/- plus 3/6d for extra lining, or £2.5/6d in all. The cuttings came home for repairs.

Initially, as we have seen in Chapter XII, law and order was preserved by the locals themselves, but later a policeman was appointed. Later still, in the days when the herring fishing and the gold rush were at their height, this was not an easy task, and three additional constables had to be brought in. There was very bitter feeling between the east and west coast fishermen. The biggest insult that could be paid, was to call an 'east coaster' a 'west coaster'. In turn, the fishermen would gang up on the shepherds, prospectors or railwaymen. With rum, whisky, and beer flowing freely on a Saturday night, fights were inevitable.

If the strict letter of the law was to be enforced, any formal charges made had to be heard in Dornoch. This was not the easiest place to reach:

even as late as 1900, this involved travelling by train to Dunrobin Station where, by arrangement with Mr McDonald, hotel keeper, Golspie, a dog cart could be waiting to take passengers to Dornoch and then bring them back to the railway. In these circumstances the officers of the law reached an unofficial agreement with the "locals" that for ordinary "drink related" offences, the local constabulary would act as arresting officers, judge, and jury. The procedure seems to have been when the sergeant and constable arrived on the scene, if the problem was a mini riot they drew their batons and waded in, but if only a mere fight was the problem, the officers stood back, waited until one was vanquished, and then took on the victor.

About this time Sergeant Anderson joined the local police force from the Morayshire force, and it is said his main recommendation had been an unofficial one that "he could fight his [not inconsiderable] weight in wildcats". Consequently, many a fight terminated in a hurry when someone shouted, "here comes the sergeant".

At least three of his successors, sergeants Gordon, MacDonald and Murray were of a like build and disposition and considered that it was a waste of time preparing reports of simple breaches of the peace. On the very few occasions that allegations were made about police assault, it seemed impossible to find witnesses prepared to testify.

As often as not, notifications of funerals were "cried" by "Hughie the Wreck" - real name now unknown - who went round the streets calling out the details. For this he usually received a fee of 5/-.

Nicknames were the rule rather than the exception. No one was missed. The dominie was "Snuffy", the Rev Dr Scott was "The Maister", John Sutherland was the "Hardy" after whom the gap in the breakwater was named, "Long Hugh" the painter who kept one of his fingernails long specially to facilitate wood graining was Hugh Findlay, and there are numerous others.

Because of the amount of time young men spent at sea, not much attention was given to sport. Some football was played, with matches against the "auld enemy" Brora maintaining their fiercely contested status (both on and off the field). The nine-hole golf course was first opened in 1859, and then again in 1946 after having been ploughed up during the Second World War.

The expense of a funeral looks very small in 1990 terms, even if the quantity of whisky drunk seems somewhat larger. On 7th February 1870 the following was spent:-

Whisky (at 16/- per gallon!)	£2.17/6d
Merchant (Mourning Clothes)	£4. 4/2 ½d
Joiner (Coffin)	£2.15/-
Baker	7/3d
Drapes	11/10 ½d

Comments on other funerals are also interesting.

In September 1869 we read that "Mrs Hill was buried on Saturday and it is said Charlie's body was raised and buried beside her".

Two funerals in December 1886 were of a different calibre as befitted the two sisters of Major General Pope who had donated the funding for the cottage hospital.

"Miss Isabella and Miss Eliza Pope, the Cottage, Navidale, both died in December and were buried at Loth. Funeral expenses for each were similar - death notices in the Northern Ensign (3/-); warning the people of Loth, Portgower and Kildonan to the funeral (13/6d); opening the grave and tolling the bell (£1); coffin and shroud (£10.10/-); Mr George Ross for refreshments at Navidale (£1.9/-); Mr John Ross for refreshments at Loth (£2.18/ 1d); railway account Helmsdale to Loth for taking Miss Eliza's corpse (10/-) and for providing 42 mourners with 3rd class return tickets at 11d each (£1.18/6d)".

In November 1887. "Jane Campbell had died suddenly at Navidale Gate." She and her father before her boarded lunatic paupers. Jane had also succeeded her father, Donald, as grass keeper for Mr Hill, Navidale, from whom she got the gate house, the ground about it and a cow's grass for her work in attending the gate and keeping back the crofters' cattle.

After the coming of the railway in 1872, concern had been expressed at the cost of living in the village. "The people in business have failed to see that ordinary mortals such as I can have equal facilities to get goods cheaply and conveniently by railway, and they have not abated their prices one copper. The consequence is that those who can afford it send south for everything, and the traders in the place only deal with the poorer class. A number of Sutherland people take their groceries from Somerville, Glasgow, who advertises largely".

The previous year one local resident had sent Somerville an order "per goods train to Golspie thence per Duke of Sutherland's Railway." It included: 20lbs tea at 2/4d per 1b, 112 lbs sugar made up in 28lb parcels at 4d per lb. - 8lbs rice at 4d per lb. - 4lbs small sago at 3d per lb. - 4lbs cornflour at 5d per lb. - 1 bottle vanilla essence at 6d. In 1874 he arranged with Somerville to send an order addressed to David Mackay, Baddanloch, Kinbrace Station, Sutherland and Caithness Railway. Mr Mackay's parcel contained: 8 bars pale soap at 3/4d per lb. - 3lbs tobacco Bogey Roll white - 3lbs tobacco Bogey Roll black - Carriage to Kinbrace was 5/6d and the whole account for Mackay's provisions was £5 2/-.

One of the gentlemen concerned had a private arrangement about butter, for in 1869 a letter went from Helmsdale to Baddanloch: "If you get an opportunity of sending my jar of butter I will consider it a favour".

A wine order went to Dymock and Guthrie, Edinburgh in 1871 for a dozen sherry at 30/- per doz.; ½ dozen port at 30/- per doz.. Whisky came from Edinburgh bottled at 16/- per gallon or from Pultneytown Distillery - four gallons at a time. Clothing, especially for special orders like mourning clothes, came partially from Hodge at Anderston Cross, Glasgow, who in 1893 supplied: 15 yds. merino at 2/6d per yd.; 5 yds. cashmere at 2/6d per yd.; 8 reels cotton No. 40 at 1d per reel; 20 yds. skirt lining at 4½d per yd.; 2 mourning veils plain with scalloped edges at 1/- each; 1 pair stay clasps 13 inches long at 4 ½d; 1 mourning bonnet full front 10/-.

Books were also ordered from afar. Mr Thin, bookseller, Edinburgh was sent 3/- in stamps and asked to supply a second-hand copy of Amsworth's Latin Dictionary. This was to be given to Menzies and Co., Edinburgh, to add to the parcel Menzies was sending to Mr Paterson, druggist, Helmsdale. In this way the book would travel free (1871).

Ink came from William Rae, Ensign Office, Wick. He was sent an empty jar which was to be filled with ink and returned to Helmsdale (1872).

Spectacles could be ordered from John McOwen, watchmaker, Crieff, who forwarded five pairs of spectacles on approbation. Four pairs were returned along with old ones for repair and 6/6d in payment "of pebbles I have kept. When you return mine please send a pair of spring ones to fold in the pocket No. 12."

Perhaps somewhat surprising is an order for a piano going to Mr Morton of Huddersfield who got a cheque for £22 10/- being the price of a piano he supplied less carriage £1 9/11d (1892).

Garden plants ordered from Howden and Co., Post Office Buildings, Inverness, with instructions to "Send per parcel post or rail whichever is cheaper", were

2 packets Sweet Alyssum
2 packets Tom Thumb Candytuft
1 packet Marigold French Double mixed
2 packets Mignonette
1 packet Phlox Drummond
2 packets Saponaria Calabrica
2 packets Virginian Stocks
1 packet Larkspur Double Dwarf Rocket
2 packets Ten week German dwarf stock.

If they all flourished one garden must have been a picture in 1889.

At one time the community did not have much success with its doctors. In April 1872 we learn "The practice sold for £250", but by 1883 the recent history of local medicine was summarised as: "We have been very unfortunate with our doctors, Dr Tulloch who went to Winnipeg had been quarrelsome, Dr Gunn had died, Dr Martin came but did not stay, and Dr MacGregor, newly appointed, had lost his wife".

The terms of engaging a domestic servant were set out in April 1892 when Maggie .... at Harpsdale Farm, Caithness, received a letter regarding her appointment. Wages were to be £5 for the first half-year with a promise of an increase if her work was satisfactory. She would be expected to take care of a cow for which there was one acre of ground, "never turnips". 1/- in stamps was enclosed as "earles" (earnest money in confirmation of her appointment), and she would be expected on the train from Halkirk with her trunk.

Coal could either be purchased in small quantities from one of the local merchants, or directly by the shipload. An example of the latter took place when a supply was ordered from Edward Eccles, Newcastle, for the local gentry and others. Mr Dudgeon (32 tons), Mr Hill (12 tons), Rev Mr McMillan (18 tons), Miss Pope (8 tons), Mrs Gunn at Culgower (10 tons), Mr Paterson (4 tons).

The coal, Wallsend Best, cost 9/- a ton and Mr Eccles was warned that the ship bringing it must not draw more than 9ft 6 inches of water to get to the harbour at Helmsdale. The people buying the coal had to arrange for carts to uplift and deliver their orders, so a letter was sent to Loth Manse (July 1883) to advise the Rev Mr McMillan that the Challenger would begin discharging that afternoon as soon as the carts arrived. The harbour weighing machine was used to make up the orders. The freight charge was £33 18/ 6d, and a guinea was given as a gratuity to the master of the ship and half a guinea "to the man keeping tally".

Strange though it may seem, the telephone was only introduced to the Post Office after 1906.

One way or another, much of what went on in the village was under the control of the Parish Council, whose decisions were often arrived at on denominational lines. Fortunately, members of one very able family were both prepared to give their time to public affairs, and to make their decisions on a rational, as opposed to a sectarian, basis. These were the Coupers.

The first member of the family mentioned in the Helmsdale records was a James Couper, farmer, who was the father of Donald Couper who died in 1881, who in turn was the father of George Couper who died in 1915. Donald, amongst other activities, had served for many years on the Parochial Board, as George did on the committee of the Harbour Trustees.

George went into business on his own and soon was in a very big way, making Stronsay the great herring centre that it was. He was also involved with various other fishing centres in England, in Scotland, and possibly in Rotterdam, and he built up a fleet of eleven steam herring drifters by 1905. Besides being directly involved with the fishing, he also seems to have had at least two other sidelines. The first was controlling the source of the direct supply of preserving salt from Spain, whilst the second was in conjunction with a firm of coal merchants and shippers in Cardiff, first known as Downing and Sutherland, and then simply Downings.

When Adam Couper died in 1933 his public interests were many and included membership of the County Council, the Education Committee, the Licensing Board, and the local School Management Committee. What is not commented on in his obituary are his large pecuniary gifts which benefited the community. These included paying off the debt burden on the harbour to the Official Receiver, so that it could then be taken over by the County Council, and his gift of the Castle Park to the village.

His father, George, who had built a very nice house on "Sandy Matheson's old croft" died in 1915, the same year as Mr James Campbell the former "Dominie", with whom he had worked very closely in the administration of the affairs of the village. Although he had resigned from his school post in 1881, Mr Campbell had continued as Session Clerk, Registrar, Inspector of the Poor and a number of other appointments until his death. Being on opposite sides of the village's religious divide meant nothing to either of them. They worked very well together - sometimes in ways which, considering their circumstances, were very, very surprising. It is only a pity that more people had not followed their example.

One letter of condolence to Mr Campbell's widow spoke of "the painstaking and accurate care with which he fulfilled his duties....especially in face of the opposition that followed the Secession of 1843". His obituaries speak of "..his extraordinary fund of stories, ...his love of all things Scottish from good porridge to bagpipe playing.....his wise and sagacious council for those with problems.... all of which would be sadly missed".

TABLE A

KILDONAN PARISH CROPS

I.	Occupiers	1866	1875	1885	1895
	(Number)	-	119	138	190
	(Renting)	-	-	-	188
		(Acres)	(Acres0	(Acres)	(Acres)
2.	Crops				
	Corn Crop				
	Barley	21	71	95	60
	Oats	48	139	283	324
	Rye	-	6	-	14
	Peas	-	6	3	1
	Green Crops				
	Potatoes	8	67	87	86
	Turnips	50	51	91	118
	Rape	-	4	-	-
	Bare Fallow Land	-	2	-	3
	Rotation Land				
	For Hay	1	73	180	225
	Not For Hay	50	324	640	255
	Permanent Grass				
	For Hay	75	3	684	63
	Not For Hay	-	29	895	951
3.	Mountain Land	-	-	-	109771
4.	Woods	-	-	-	150

NB. Criteria have varied over the years, so the above
figures are not always comparable the one with the other.

TABLE B

LOTH PARISH CROPS

1. Occupiers	1866	1875	1885	1895
(Number)	-	40	45	47
(Renting)	-	-	-	46
	(Acres)	(Acres)	(Acres)	(Acres)
2. Crops				
Corn Crop				
Wheat	6	-	-	-
Barley	152	198	151	132
Oats	270	270	280	253
Rye	-	6	-	-
Green Crops				
Potatoes	19	49	38	36
Turnips	202	223	102	183
Cabbage	-	1	2	3
Bare Fallow Land	-	6	4	-
Rotation Land				
Not for Hay	477	161	170	32
For Hay	-	150	198	162
Permanent Grass				
Not For Hay	8	5	8	230
For Hay	85	153	158	225
3. Mountain Land	-	-	-	14659
4. Woods	-	-	-	35

NB. Criteria have varied over the years, so the above
figures are not always comparable the one with the other.

TABLE C
KILDONAN PARISH FARMSTOCKS

	1866	1875	1885	1895
I. Occupiers				
(Number)	-	119	138	190
(Renting)	-	-	-	188
2. Livestock				
Cattle				
Milk Cows	229	168	184	229
Others				
Over 2 yrs	65	45	33	37
Under 2 yrs	66	90	85	195
Sheep				
Over 1 year	15373	11458	12159	12407
Under 1 year	837	4523	5440	5944
Pigs	126	35	44	63
Poultry				
Turkeys	-	-	18	-
Geese	-	-	10	-
Ducks	-	-	23	-
Fowls	-	-	666	-
Horses				
Farm Use	-	68	83	123
Unbroken	-	15	19	16
Animals died				
or slaughtered				
Cattle	-	-	8	-
Sheep	-	-	348	-
Pigs	-	-	22	-

N.B. Criteria have varied over theyears, so the above figures
are not always comparable, the one with the other.

TABLE D
LOTH PARISH FARMSTOCKS

		1866	1875	1885	1895
I.	Occupiers				
	(Number)	-	-	-	47
	(Renting)	-	-	-	46
2.	Livestock				
	Cattle				
	Milk Cows	81	80	125	84
	Others				
	Over 2 yrs	107	189	92	62
	Under 2 yrs	66	78	-	97
	Sheep				
	Over 1 year	1817	6641	2430	2832
	Under 1 year	1111	2343	1212	1597
	Pigs	53	35	30	27
	Poultry				
	Turkeys	-	-	14	-
	Geese	-	-	3	-
	Ducks	-	-	54	-
	Fowls	-	-	344	-
	Horses				
	Farm Use	-	53	46	56
	Unbroken	-	14	15	5
	Animals died or slaughtered				
	Cattle	-	-	4	-
	Sheep	-	-	31	-
	Pigs	-	-	17	-

N.B. Criteria have varied over theyears, so the above figures
are not always comparable, the one with the other.

TABLE E
TABLE OF ANNUAL HELMSDALE IMPORTS
1831-1865

Year	Bale Gds B.B.	Porter & Ale Hhd.	Oats Bolls	Barley Tons	Lime Tons	Coals Tons	Salt Tons
1831	524	61	587	193	-	339	971
1832	354	18	601	195	-	134	773
1833	481	17	680	292	-	467	386
1834	200	6	800	2078	134	273	909
1835	271	6	782	367	30	255	377
1836	451	9	990	789	-	175	701
1837	411	4	264	657	50	497	816
1838	704	25	668	733	535	396	1234
1839	1488	11	1638	308	233	394	404
1840	1564	73	1348	577	95	900	20
1841		NO INFORMATION					
1842		NO INFORMATION					
1843	909	43	1046	170	108	469	-
1844	849	34	1734	-	197	390	-
1845	845	34	1528	133	85	324	-
1846	767	34	1162	-	248	469	3
1847	607	30	1411	155	-	184	-
1848	1164	60	1687	382	251	536	-
1849	923	10	1656	394	27	378	85
1850	848	35	2188	899	113	511	-
1851	669	16	1706	441	216	358	2
1852	854	30	1735	366	91	602	-
1853	1216	19	2230	165	60	201	32
1854	797	32	1709	151	112	485	178
1855	1164	45	1875	220	40	559	-
1856	849	69	2661	-	125	536	99
1857	923	43	2996	804	120	592	35
1858	1421	67	3099	756	28	646	10
1859	990	35	2108	282	74	545	17
1860	884	51	2355	2	71	612	7
1861	1054	53	2678	-	-	974	12
1862	1314	52	2349	-	41	788	83
1863	1163	18	1304	-	22	462	4
1864	1509	51	1433	-	90	610	150
1865	1555	47	1024	4	90	735	121

TABLE F

TABLE OF ANNUAL HELMSDALE EXPORTS
1831-1865

Year	Wheat	Barley	Beans & Peas	Wool	Aqua	Salmon		Herring	Haddocks	Boats	
	Qrs	Qrs.	Qrs	Sts	Punch	Box	Kit.	Barls.	Barls	Home	Callg
1831	132	-	25	2360	57	541	150	14306	-	128	6
1832	67	167	46	2219	55	1005	83	4931	-	30	12
1833	20	352	40	1809	36	987	128	15892	-	111	14
1834	149	-	10	-	28	819	-	6901	-	102	-
1835	161	73	10	2678	82	971	-	16514	-	121	-
1836	113	81	61	1779	50	576	-	12671	-	157	16
1837	65	-	-	-	63	434	-	29237	-	165	-
1838	-	-	-	1943	63	402	-	29363	-	186	3
1839	15	-	-	2005	25	299	-	36116	-	215	12
1840	15	160	4	-	109	237	44	22196	-	224	28
1841	NO INFORMATION										
1842	NO INFORMATION										
1843	71	871	-	3451	-	312	36	30729	-	235	17
1844	-	631	-	1755	-	297	55	20832	-	244	20
1845	68	1488	-	2898	-	433	56	16637	-	231	19
1846	62	1194	-	2126	-	450	97	17487	-	213	19
1847	128	806	-	4094	-	434	27	24258	-	162	19
1848	74	904	-	2690	-	437	42	25028	-	178	33
1849	47	1500	-	3070	-	285	182	20160	-	146	16
1850	24	155	-	1868	-	-	-	18479	-	117	12
1851	7	1190	-	1894	-	-	-	19898	-	131	16
1852	-	1376	-	2407	-	-	-	14075	-	144	16
1853	-	859	-	2016	-	-	-	19190	965	151	25
1854	113	1033	-	6434	-	-	-	19711	-	141	23
1855	-	81	20	1265	-	-	-	22270	-	161	17
1856	16	862	-	2796	-	-	-	18493	1665	175	16
1857	-	1509	-	1396	-	-	-	23115	855	206	-
1858	-	1467	-	3487	-	-	-	16959	686	233	21
1859	20	534	-	4836	-	-	-	11402	216	213	17
1860	8	401	-	3092	-	-	-	19473	101	189	28
1861	-	361	-	3060	-	-	-	26772	202	211	17
1862	-	475	-	2894	-	-	-	31888	2	258	9
1863	-	300	-	3363	-	-	-	27037	19	242	12
1864	-	411	-	2517	-	-	-	38037	28	245	11
1865	-	252	-	2420	-	-	-	14259	74	283	32

TABLE G

HELMSDALE HERRING CATCHES 1814-42

YEAR	BARRELS	YEAR	BARRELS
1814	2,400	1829	13,929
1815	4,000	1830	18,169
1816	7,300	1831	15,551
1817	9,350	1832	6,332
1818	14,390	1833	20,263
1819	20,060	1834	6,136
1820	18,835	1835	21,639
1821	18,780	1836	15,193
1822	19,300	1837	29,800
1823	21,215	1838	38,400
1824	23,692	1839	38,754
1825	23,450	1840	28,500
1826	9,805	1841	39,504
1827	19,030	1842	28,271
1828	12,712		

TABLE H
TABLE OF ANNUAL HELMSDALE IMPORTS
1880 - 1889

Year	Bale Goods B.B	Porter & Ale Hhd.	Barley Tons	Lime Tons	Coals Tons	Salt Tons	Slate Tons	Cement Tons	Herring Barrels
1880	-	-	-	1612	884	1176	-	-	-
1881	-	241	-	482	1257	991	34	-	130
1882	300	383	166	834	1113	1224	12	25	-
1883	24	120	84	308	1154	785	40	-	44
1884	-	-	-	74	1173	656	-	-	-
1885	-	-	-	45	1178	422	202	8	-
1886	-	-	-	-	1228	878	-	-	-
1887	-	-	-	-	1046	817	40	-	-
1888	-	-	-	75	1187	1062	55	-	-
1889	-	-	-	-	1087	1458	13	-	48

TABLE J
TABLE OF ANNUAL HELMSDALE EXPORTS
1880 - 1889

	By Sea		By Rail					
			Cod &			White		
	Herrings	Herrings	Ling	Crabs	Lobsters	Fish	Boats	
Year	Barrels	Cran	Cwt	Cwt		Cwt	Home	Calling
1880	9645	-	-	-	-	-	173	375
1881	14104	-	-	-	-	-	146	289
1882	5924	-	-	-	-	-	169	210
1883	6604	-	-	-	-	-	107	43
1884	5469	-	-	-	-	-	83	68
1885	11126	-	-	-	-	-	78	27
1886	11406	-	-	-	-	-	85	84
1887	15934	776	1616	5700	2850	2113	83	52
1888	22117	336	2425	9000	1809	2870	96	73
1889	18060	548	3744	9300	1450	1719	118	73

TABLE K
LISTS OF CHURCH MINISTERS OR READERS
Parish of Kildonan

1567	Andrew Bain	1766	William Keith
1574	Andrew Anderson and Philip Anderson	1787	Alexander Sage
1577	George Ruthven	1824	James Campbell
1584	William Livingston	1845	William McKillican
1602	Walter Anderson	1848	Alex MacDonald
1641	Gabriel Maxwell	1866	James MacPherson
1656	Andrew Anderson	1867	Partick Clark
1673	James Hay	1875	Daniel Fraser
1712	Alexander Brodie	1894	Archibald Black Scott
1725	William Rose	1948	John S Fulton
1740	Hugh Sutherland	1978	Graham R Houston
1755	Hugh Ross	1982	John Rushton
1761	John Ross	1996	Melvin Griffiths

Parish of Loth

1567	Andrew Anderson	1782	James Gilchrist
1627	William Cumming	1739	William Rose
1634	James Thomson	1756	George McCulloch
1640	Hector Munro	1802	George Gordon
1656	John Rose	1823	Donald Ross
1669	George Gray	1848	Duncan St. Clair
1682	Hector Paip (Pope)	1861	Gilbert McMillan
1721	Robert Robertson	1903	James S. M. Mowat
		1922	Robert L. MacNie

(Parish divided between parishes of Clyne and of Kildonan in 1927.)

Helmsdale United Free Church
(Christian Names not Known)

1900	A Grant	1935	D J McInnes
1906	J Cameron	1937	N MacKenzie-White
1911	M Munro	1939	R MacAskill
1929	A McCall	1947/48	United with St John's

Helmsdale Free Church

1843	John MacDonald	1936	Malcolm MacDonald
1856	Robert Finlayson	1942	Murdo Nicolson
1862	Alex Murchison	1955	Joseph Perry
1878	D M MacRae	1968	Kenneth Stone
1889	A Grant	1983	Duncan MacLeod
1907	A M Ross		

TABLE L
SELECTED DETAILS OF GAME BAGS
ON BORROBOL ESTATE, SUTHERLANDSHIRE

YEAR	GROUSE (brace)	STAGS (Red)	ROD-CAUGHT SALMON (Spring fish only)	
1876	78	6	48	
1877	568	6	118	
1878	1280	5	124	
1879	1602	4	27	
1880	2106	4	27	
1881	1769	5	57	
1882	1	7	50	
1883	13	8	151	
1884	196	9	198	
1939	460 ½	14	N/A	War-time years
1940	521	4	N/A	Little sport
1941	326	8	N/A	used.
1942	48	1	N/A	
1943	116 ½	10	N/A	
1945	18 ½	12	N/A	
1946	46 ½	3	N/A	
1965	190	35		No salmon
1966	261	35		details known.
1967	313	35		
1968	208	60		(All-terrain vehicles
1969	359	32		come into operation)
1976	93	50		
1977	82	59		
1978	175	60		
1979	136	60		
1980	181	70		
1985	147	55	411	Jan - Sept
1986	42	66	456	figures,
1987	124 ½	66	377	full season.
1988	185	80	411	
1989	345 ½	81	367	
1990	378	70	388	
1991	236	72	299	
1992	102	71	663	
1993	21	84	410	
1994	0	91	436	
1995	0	85	506	

TABLE M

HEALTH AND OTHER PROBLEMS
AFFECTING SCHOOL ATTENDANCES

1.   Starting with epidemics and health problems we have

1870   Almost panic at Parish school due to fever.
1882   Outbreak of Scarlet Fever.
1890   Epidemics of influenza and whooping cough.
1892   Scarlet fever epidemic - school closes for four weeks.
1892   Influenza epidemic - school closes for three weeks.
1897   Whooping Cough prevalent - school closed for three weeks.
1901   Closed for three weeks on account of measles.
1903   School closes for two weeks - influenza outbreak.
1909   School attendances affected by mumps (40), and herring
          fishing at Wick and Shetlands (20).
1910   School closes for disinfection (diphtheria).
1911   School troubled by chickenpox and ringworm.
1913   H.G. school closes for two days to allow attendance at Inverness
          Mod, and four weeks for whooping cough!
1918   School closed for 3 weeks because of influenza and whooping cough.

2.   Other factors causing absenteeism were:-

1864   Herring fishing, harvesting and Brora market.
1875   School attendance irregularity very disheartening - causes
          include market on Thursdays, and Annual Review
          (of volunteers) at Dunrobin.
1901   School attendance in June affected by families going to
          fishing and to cut peats.
1904   School attendance affected by families going to fishing,
          children gathering whelks, or helping at peat cutting.
1905   Whelk gathering "much in evidence" amongst absentees.
1908   30 children away at herring fishing.
1914   65 children go to fishing at Wick and Shetland.

TABLE N
EXTRACTS FROM SCHOOL LOG BOOKS

1854   Mr James Campbell, teacher at General Assembly
        School in Helmsdale appointed Parochial Schoolmaster of Kildonan.

1859   School fees of £2 12/2d paid for pauper's children.

1864   Parochial School has a roll of 103 of whom 64 are from Free Church homes.

1866   New Year's Day Jan 12th; fast held for cattle plague;
        teaching difficulties from scarcity of books; stormiest day since 1851.

1867   Parochial Schoolmaster's remuneration:-

Salary	£35	0s 0d
Allowance in lieu of garden	2	2s 0d
Allnce. in aid of Gov grant	7	0s 0d
	£59	2s 0d (£59.10p)

1869   Schoolhouse condemned by inspector as unfit for living in
        - to be repaired.

1872   Most of "big boys" leaving school employed as "nippers" on railway.
        Scottish Education Act becomes law. As a result Parish School
        is to be called Helmsdale East school and Free Church school
        becomes Helmsdale West school.
        (Locally known as "moderates" school and "Free" school respectively.)

1873   Schools observe 1st January as holiday for first time.

1876   Scarcity of books tells on work of teachers.

1877   Five panes of glass of "East school" broken by "strange children - i.e. not
        belonging to this school". The head teacher dispatches a group of "haflins" to
        "identify" offenders. Treatment seems to have been effective as incident is not
        repeated!

1881   Mr J Campbell East School headmaster resigns "because
        of underhand work in parish as regards to education".
        He is succeeded by Mr J Matheson.
        Helmsdale Free Church school closes, and pupils
        transferred to Helmsdale East school. Former Free
        Church school at Portgower continues.

1884   Number on Parish school roll is 252 but in January the
        average attendance was 151 in May and 108 in September.

1887	Parish School has to be closed on Jan 12th because of continuing local observance of "old" New Year.
	Holiday for Queen's Jubilee - fountain to be erected "opposite Post Office"..
1888	School gets supply of writing slates "as many younger children do not bring them".
1889	School fees abolished.
1891	Mr J Munro is appointed as headmaster. "247 in attendance...probably highest attendance in history of school....I endeavour to get on without corporal punishment, but attempt has failed...".
1892	"Water scarcity tends to appal the most callous amongst us".
1895	Dispute with parents of children at side school having to provide teacher with free accommodation.
1897	Queen Victoria's Diamond Jubilee celebrated with treats for children in Battery Park.
1900	School gets half holiday for Queen's birthday and Relief of Mafeking.
1902	Coronation of King Edward VII celebrated with treats for children in Battery Park by kind permission of Mr Donald Mackay, harbourmaster.
1905	Mrs Egerton gives annual treat in Drill Hall.
1906	School science class visits local carpet factory.
1907	School Board write Mr James Coates Jr thanking him for gift of bookcase and books.
	School staffing difficulties because teacher's family affected by diphtheria
1908	Mr Taylor, Salscraggie, gives treat for children (picnic and games) at Caen.
	One stormy day only 20 children arrive at school.
	Start made to provision of lunch time cocoa for (30 country) school children.
	Jas Coates Jr of Paisley provides school bags for all pupils.
	Death of Edward VII - school closed.
	40 children go to fishing at Wick and Shetlands.
	Mr W. Munro appointed head teacher - roll 212.
1913	Dental examination reveals all children have bad teeth, and 20 have four or more.
	Dentist visits school - over 100 pupils need extractions.
	When dentist returns to school there are large number of absences, especially amongst girls.
	Diphtheria amongst head teacher's family - school closed for a week and all jotters etc. burned.
1915	Over 100 pupils absent on December 6th because of wind and torrential rain.
	School Boards abolished - become Education Authorities.
1919	Increasing amount of bad attendance because of toothache.

1920	Water heating installed in Infant Room at school, but in spite of this temperatures at 9.30 a.m. on 6th December were 38, 44, 39, 43, 41 - all degrees Farenheight.
1923	Torrish side school still operating.
1929	Education Authorities become committees of County Councils.
1930	School log entries reveal Torrish Side School still operating; new gymnasium opened; and measles epidemic raging.
1933	School closes for Mod at Brora. Scarlet fever and impetigo raging.
1935	School holiday for Silver Jubilee celebrations, children march to Couper Park.School upgraded to Senior Secondary.
1936	Soup kitchen opens at school - 60 children supplied daily.
1938	82 exclusions for mumps (including headmaster!).
1939	Twenty city war time evacuees join school roll.
1940	New school kitchen opens.
1943	Side school in use at Elderable.
1944	40 pupils helped farmers with harvest.
1945	(January 18th) Snow feet deep everywhere. Mr J. Cook takes over as headteacher. Lunch time snacks now soup instead of cocoa.
1946	School collects 63 lbs. of rosehips for hospital.
1948	School downgraded to Junior Secondary - roll now 178 (38 in secondary); 29 cases of mumps; new work room at school brought into commission.
1950	School heating improved by addition of slow combustion stoves, and new dining room erected.
1951	Charge for school meals raised from 5d to 6d; 192 food parcels presented to school from Fiji Islands; Wireless set installed at school; and 27 pupils from school sent to potato gathering.
1953	Coronation memento for each pupil to be New Testament and carton of sweets. Discussions start as to colour scheme for new school.
1954	Four school boys have impetigo.
1955	Severe storm and frost closes school in January and February. New school opens (April 13th).
1957	Polio injections given to children
1959	Mr D J Bates new headmaster.
1960	Sign of staff outlook when cleaner stops cleaning in middle of job when asked to carry water.
1962	Secondary pupils transferred to Golspie school.
1986	School becomes a primary.
Note:	These extracts are based on notes made from the Log Books by Mr A I Blance, head teacher from 1968 -86. The books themselves are now in the custody of the Highland Council Archivist at Inverness.

BIBLIOGRAPHY

I Primary Sources

Scottish Record Office references AD14/17/2, AF25, AF39, AF58, CH2, CS96, CS279, GDS, JC26/383; National Library of Scotland Ref ACC313, ACC10225, and ACC10853, all archives of Sutherland Estates papers; Archives of late James Campbell and late J D (Hamish) Campbell; Records of Sutherland County Council, its statutory predecessors, and its statutory successors; Minute books of the Helmsdale Lifeboat Association, Parish Church of St. John, Bunillidh Church of Scotland, Helmsdale Free Church and of Helmsdale United Free Church.

II Secondary Sources

An Account of the Improvements on the Estates of the Marquess of Stafford by James Loch; Mr A I Blance notes on school log books; Dear Duchess by Denis Stewart; Berwick- upon-Tweed Directory 1928, Parson and White; Donnan the Great and his Munntier, by Rev Dr A B Scott; Glasgow's Celtic Church by Ian R MacDonald; Gloomy Memories, 1899 Edition, Donald Macleod; Highland Locomotives by Peter Tatlow; The Highland Railway, by H A Vallance; The Highland Railway Journal; History of Berwick-upon-Tweed, Fuller 1799; History of Berwick-upon-Tweed and its Vicinity 1817, Rev Thomas Johnstone; Journals of the Episcopal   visitations of the Rt Rev Robert Forbes to the dioceses of Ross and Caithness 1762, (Ed) Ven J B Grower 1884; The Leviathan of Wealth, Eric Richards; North Railway Magazine, James Loch and the House of Sutherland 1812-1855, Unpublished Ph D Thesis by Eric Richards; The Life of the Celtic Church by James Balloch; Looking Back, Autobiography of 5th Duke of Sutherland; Memorabilia Domestica by Donald Sage; New Ways Through the Glens by A R B Haldane; Northern Times Newspaper, Golspie; Sailing Drifters, by Edgar G March; A Salmon Saga: the Story of the Berwick Salmon Fisheries Company Ltd 1856-1956; Scottish Volunteer Force by J M Grierson; The Sea Fisheries of Scotland by James R Coull; Statistical Accounts of   Parishes of Loth and of Kildonan; Sutherland Estate Management, R J Adam Editor; The Volunteer Artillery by Litchfield and Westlake.

INDEX